The Higher Christian Life

How to Attain Faith and Joy Through the Lord Jesus Christ

By W. E. Boardman

Adansonia
Press

Published in 2018

Logo art adapted from work by Bernard Gagnon

ISBN-13: 978-1-387-99848-7

First published in 1858

Contents

Preface iv

Part One - What It Is 6
    Chapter One - The Book Wanted 6
    Chapter Two - Historical Example 7
    Chapter Three - Examples Compared 12
    Chapter Four - Explanations 17
    Chapter Five - A Stumbling Stone 24
    Chapter Six - Not For Me? Why Not? 28

Part Two - How Attained 36
    Chapter One - For Me: What Then Must I Do? 36
    Chapter Two - Christ All-Sufficient and Faith All-Inclusive 46
    Chapter Three - Stopped In The Way 55
    Chapter Four - The Way Missed 63

Part Three - Progress and Power 74
    Chapter One - Stages of Progress 74
    Chapter Two - Times and Seasons 83
    Chapter Three - The Present and the Future 87
    Chapter Four - The Christian Life 96
    Chapter Five - The Contrast 103
    Chapter Six - The Harmony 109
    Chapter Seven - Gathering Power of the Church Foreshadowed ... 119
    Chapter Eight - Closing Counsels and Parting Words 124

Preface

The title-page will suffice the careless one; he will go no farther. The curious will go deeper, and a little patience and perseverance will satisfy him also, and perhaps repay him for his time and trouble. If the earnest searcher for the best things can be satisfied as fully, he will be repaid a thousand fold, and the great aim of the book will be gained.

In unfolding the subject, the historical and inductive method has been chosen, both as the most interesting and convincing. Examples of experience are given from history as a basis — in connexion with the Bible — but beyond that, sketches from life, never before published, have been preferred, because of their freshness, and also for the purpose of adding to the treasures of published Christian experience. Lovers of truth cannot fail to be profited by the mass of facts embodied, even though they should dissent from the inductions of the author.

The Higher Christian Life, as a title has been adopted for want of a better. A wider sphere for the experimental truth set forth, and a clearer delineation are the things sought; and hackneyed terms, or pre-appropriated terms, or terms against which prejudice is arrayed, would not answer.

Next after this title "Full trust and Full Salvation" would have been preferred, as most expressive and least objectionable. Full trust, rather than full faith, because, faith has been so philosophised into a hundred shades of meaning, and so hackneyed in use as, to have lost its significance to many. Trust is perhaps the only other word that conveys the original meaning of faith. And as faith is the all inclusive condition of salvation, full trust expresses the sole condition of full salvation which it is the design of this volume to illustrate.

Jesus is the way. Full trust the means. Therefore — to secure confidence in Jesus, if possible — it has been the author's great aim to develop, clearly, fully, and simply, the relations of Jesus to the soul, and of the soul to Jesus.

In the use of terms the Bible principle — not the strict one — has been followed. "Second Conversion" for example. Of course, it is not intended, to convey the idea of a second regeneration, but that expressed by President Edwards, in the term — "Remarkable Conversions," —- which is the title of his account of several remarkable cases of higher life attained after conversion.

Such "conversions" are certainly "remarkable "but if there are any who think the experience beyond the reach of all, let them try it by the Word — the only infallible criterion — if it is not warranted by the Bible, reject it; but if it stands the test, then seize it as a treasure above rubies. And if any believe in the truth of this matter, but would like other terms, and other methods, let them bear in mind that while truth is one, methods are many; and if experimental truth is taught and received, it is of very little consequence whether theories and terms to which we are accustomed, are associated with it or not.

If it is God's truth, fitly spoken, and has His blessing, it will stand; otherwise let it fall to the ground.

Part One - What It Is

Chapter One - The Book Wanted

"PREPARE YE THE WAY OF THE PEOPLE." — ISAIAH LXII. 10.

Some disciples of Christ live, life-long, under condemnation, and know no better. They are always doubting, and think they must always doubt. And very many live a life of ups and downs, and suppose that to be the best God has in store for them while in the body. Occasionally they gain some lookout in the mount, and then, through the swaying branches of the trees of life moved by the breath of heaven, they catch glimpses of the river of the waters of life, gleaming in the rays of the Sun of Righteousness, and are filled with gladness. But then again, soon they find themselves in the low grounds of unbelief, wrapped up in fogs of doubt, and chilled, and poisoned, by the mist and malaria of worldly cares and worldly company. To all these, a book which should bring the knowledge, as really reliable and true, that there is actually, a sunny side of the Christian life — such an experimental knowledge of Jesus, as. would place the soul, as a vineyard on the southern slope, under the sun and the rain of heaven, to blossom and ripen its luscious fruit in abundance for the glory of the Master — Ah, how such a book would be hailed as glad tidings from God!

Many have heard or read upon this subject, and do really believe there is something better than they have found, but are afraid. They are convinced that there is something in it, but they fear to try to find out what it is. They are earnest Christians too, and would gladly go on out of the wilderness of doubt and perplexity if they dared to venture. They see that there is a land of milk and honey offered by the promises of God, and would press for it, but alas, the spies bring back a bad report of the land, "Hard to gain," say they. "Cities walled up to heaven. Giants in the land, sons of Anak." "Hard to keep, even if conquered." Fear chimes in with this, and so they shrink back. Or they fear heresy and wildfire. So much has been written about " perfection" and " sanctification" in conflict with the Bible and church standards, and so many have made shipwreck, and run wild, that the spectres of grim and ghastly errors rise up to affright them from the very first step. Now a book which should clearly point out what is warranted by the Bible and the standards, and show it in plain and full contrast with what is condemned by them, would be hailed by such persons as an angel messenger from heaven, beckoning them onward and upward to the land of Beulah.

A few, at least, probably more than any one knows or thinks, are convinced, and feeling after something they scarce know what, whatever it is, set before them; but they move fearfully, spectres affright and hinder, but do not wholly stop them. Or if they urge their way regardless of these, their struggles are wearisome and vain. Often and often they put forth the hand to touch the spring of the door, to admit the light, but alas, the hand finds only the cold dead wall and recoils from it with a chill, only to be stretched forth again and again, to be withdrawn in disappointment. With what untold joy, would these struggling, groping ones, receive and devour a book which should show up to them, the Way, the Truth, the Life, and point out also the many false ways they must avoid to gain the true, and walk in it!

Some have already found the way, and are glad journeyers therein. They are on the sunny side; they have gained the heights of Beulah, and delight in everything that relates to it. They would rejoice in anything defining to them distinctly the relations of this blessed Christian life to further Christian progress, and to all Christian duty. And moreover, they would be thankful to God for a Book, which they could safely put into the hands of others, hopeful of good, fearless of evil. One they could heartily commend as unfolding the fullness of the blessings of the Gospel, without feeling under the necessity of cautioning and warning against false theories, wrong terms, or evil tendencies.

The Book wanted, therefore, in this department of sacred literature, is one that will set forth the truth as it is, with the clear ring of the fearless silver trumpet, in no uncertain sound.

Whether this shall prove the Book wanted, God knoweth, time will show, and the reader will judge.

Chapter Two - Historical Example

"LIFT UP A STANDARD FOR THE PEOPLE." — ISAIAH LXII. 10.

The Bible abounds in examples. In God's Holy Word sin and holiness come up and pass on before us in living forms, rather than in abstract teachings. Truth and falsehood are first lived out, and then recorded for the world's instruction. The mercies and judgments of God are set before us in striking examples. The rescue of Noah saved amidst the desolations of a world drowned in the flood; Lot, delivered from the devouring fires which laid in ashes Sodom and Gomorrah; the children of Israel passing the Red Sea dry-shod and safe, while Pharaoh and his host sank as lead in the mighty waters; these things have filled the world with their report and taught all nations their lessons. Men and nations are raised up, live out their life, and die, and their history is written to live forever. Lessons taught in this way strike out and traverse the globe, and strike home never to be forgotten. There is no treatise upon faith like the simple story of Abraham's life: none upon patience like the story of Job: none upon courage like the story of Daniel: none upon meekness like the life of Moses: none upon zeal like the life of Paul: none upon love like the story of Job. This is God's method, and the best.

Take a few examples of The Higher Life, or Full Trust and Full Salvation. First,

MARTIN LUTHER.

When a little boy, Martin carried the faggots for his father, John Luther, to kindle the fire in his little iron smelting furnace, in Germany, God designed him to become the bearer of fuel for his own groat fire of the Reformation, to smelt the hearts of millions and re-cast the life of the world. But as yet this boy's own heart and his own life were in the crude and corrupt state of nature, hard and unmaleable as the ore of the mine and as full of impurities, to be expelled only by the fires of Divine love. His mother loved and pitied and indulged him, but his father was severe and never spared the rod. That he was not an angel in his youth we may know, for he tells of himself that he was whipped fifteen times in one day in his first school. But all this did not beat grace into his heart, though it may have beaten letters into his head. He made brilliant progress in study, and at twenty years of age received his degree at the university as a Bachelor of Arts. Up to this time his heart was in the world. His father designed him for the law, and his own ambition no doubt aspired to the honors within easy reach in that line of life. God designed otherwise. Just at that critical time when the very next step would be the first in a life-long profession, one of his fellow students dear to him as a brother beloved, one Alexis, was assassinated. The report of this tragic affair coming to Luther's ear, he hurried to the spot and found it even so. Often before, conscience, and the spirit in his heart, had urged him to a religious life, in preparation for death and the judgment. And now, as he stood gazing upon the bloody corpse of his dear friend Alexis, and thought how in a moment, prepared or unprepared, he had been summoned from earth, he asked himself the question, "What would become of me if I were thus suddenly called away?"

This was in A. D. 1505, in summer. Taking advantage of the summer's vacation, Luther, now in his twenty-first year, paid a visit to Mansfeldt the home of his infancy. Even then the purpose of a life of devotion was forming in his heart, but not yet ripened into full and final decision. The only life of religion known to him, and at all meeting his convictions, was that of the convent, the life of a monk and a priest. Whether it was because the purpose was only yet in embryo, or because he dreaded his father's displeasure, or shrunk from dashing his father's hopes and giving him pain, it seems he kept the matter back. The fire burned on in his own breast, but the young Bachelor of Arts kept it hidden, even from those most deeply interested in him of all upon earth.

On his way back to the university, however, he was overtaken by a terrific storm. "The thunder roared," says D'Aubigne; "a thunderbolt sunk into the ground by his side; Luther threw himself on his knees; his hour is perhaps come. Death, judgment, eternity, are before him in all their terrors, and speak with a voice which he can no longer resist. 'Encompassed with the anguish and terror of death,' as he says of himself, 'he makes a vow, if God will deliver him from this danger, to forsake the world, and devote himself to his service.' Risen from the earth, having still before his eyes that death must one day overtake him, he examines himself seriously, and inquires what he must do. The thoughts that formerly troubled him returned with redoubled power. He has endeavored, it is true, to fulfill all his duties. But what is the state of his soul? Can he, with a polluted soul, appear before the tribunal of so terrible a God? He must become holy"— for this he will go into the cloister, he will enter a convent, he will become a monk and a priest in the Augustinian order. He will there become holy and be saved.

This scene has been compared to that on the Damascus road centuries before, and they are not without certain similarities, both in the men, and in the circumstances and results. But there were broad differences: for while Saul of Tarsus was relieved of his blindness after only three days of darkness and desolation, Luther had yet before him months and months of monastic groping, before his eyes were opened to receive the Lord Jesus as the All in All. And while at the word of Ananias the scales fell from the eyes of the young devotee of Judaism at once, in a moment — the eyes of the young devotee of Romanism were opened, not entirely at the first touch of the Master's fingers, but rather like him who first saw only men as trees walking, and afterwards, when touched again, saw clearly.

It was a terrible blow to his parents when Luther entered the convent at Erfurth, and an astonishment to all his friends, and, as it proved in the end, a painful experiment, and a vain one, to gain salvation. Christ alone could pardon sin, but Luther had that yet to learn. He thought to merit salvation. Christ alone is the sinner's righteousness and sanctification, but he fully believed the way to become holy and just, was to shut himself up within holy walls, amongst a holy brotherhood, and perform holy offices. God designed him to be the foremost reformer of the Church, and therefore led him through all the processes of the Church, to show him their emptiness and vanity: led him at last to Rome itself and made him see the blasphemous hollowness of all its ceremonies, and the vile corruption of the men he held in such veneration. But it is no part of our design now to follow him though all this wearisome course, or to recount the painful revelations of vanity and corruption made to him step by step as he was led along. It is rather with Luther's experience as a Christian than as a Reformer, that our present purpose is concerned. The object before us is to see how the Lord brought him out of bondage into liberty, and out of darkness into light, and brought him at last out of church processes, and out of the ways of his own devising, to take the a Lord Jesus as the all in all, rather than to show how he was trained to break the bondage and dispel the darkness of an enslaved and benighted church.

Buried in the convent at Erfurth he toiled and suffered two terrible years in vain for salvation. He became emaciated, pale, hollow-eyed, downcast, hopeless. The lovely and noble Staupitz, Vicar General and head of the Augustine order in Thuringia, was the first to shed any ray of light upon the dark and troubled mind of Luther. Staupitz pointed Luther to the word of God and to the grace of Christ, and inspired him with some gleams of hope that hope might some time be his. But although the floods of wrath from the windows of heaven were stayed, and. the fountains of hell from beneath were closed, the waters gone over him had not yet subsided, the dove of peace found yet no resting place in his soul, and the bow of the covenant of promise had not yet sprung forth to his view. Indeed his struggles and watchings and fastings brought him to the brink of the grave. He was seized with an illness that threatened his life. One day a venerable monk came into his cell. Luther opened his heart to him. Despair had seized upon him. The pains of hell got hold of him. The good old man pointed him to his credo. Luther had learned the apostle's creed in his childhood, and had said it over thousands of times, but when the monk repeated to him in the tones of a sincere faith the words, "I believe in the forgiveness of sins," they carried a light and a consolation, never before felt, to the sufferer's soul. "Ah!" said the monk, "you must believe not merely that David's sins or Peter's are forgiven; the devils believe that. The commandment of God is, that we believe our own sins are forgiven. St. Bernard says, in his discourse on the annunciation, 'The testimony of the Holy Ghost to your heart is Thy sins are forgiven thee."

Luther believed, and joy filled his soul. He rose quickly from the depths of despair and from the bed of sickness. Life from the dead was given him in a two-fold sense. The forgiveness of sins was ever after a living article in his faith, and not a dead letter in the apostles' creed. He knew and was a witness to others that the greatest sinner may be forgiven. But as yet, the great underlying principle of justification by faith, was to him one of the deep and hidden things of God. The noble Staupitz and the good old Monk already before him, knew as much as Luther had now learned, and more. And all this Luther himself might have known, and yet lived a monk all his days. But God had greater things in store for him, and greater lessons to teach him. All this and more he might have taught life-long, with the burning zeal of a Paul, and the commanding eloquence of an Apollos, without causing the foundation of Rome to tremble, or freeing the church from a single fetter or chain, and without even enjoying himself, the liberty of the children of God, or the blessings of full trust and full salvation. Mark what follows.

The assassination of the dear Alexis had awakened him. The thunderbolt on the Erfurth road struck the death blow of his indecision, and Staupitz and the good Monk with his credo and his faith, had shed the first rays and comforts of salvation upon his pathway. This was all they could do. For all this God used them, but now he was about to make his own Holy word the means of leading Luther out into the light, and onward into the open field of truth not yet reached by either the prelate or the monk. Luther had no Bible. He had access to one in Latin chained to a stone pillar in the convent, a striking emblem of the Bible at that day. Locked up in a dead language, and chained to a cold monastic pillar of dead stone. And yet thank God neither itself dead nor yet bound. Another Bible he could see also in the Latin by going to the library of the University to read it. That was the first copy of the Bible he ever saw, and the first word of the Bible he ever read, from the Bible itself, was the story of Hannah and her child Samuel lent to the Lord forever, and this charmed him. Yet another copy of the sacred word was within his reach by going to a brother monk's cell to read it, in Latin also. A Bible all his own, was a prize too great for his fondest dreams. And yet God gave him one. Staupitz brought him a Bible, a Latin Bible, and presented it to him to be all his own. O, what a treasure. How eagerly he searched it. What delight it gave him. That was the first stone of his great work. That Latin Bible was all his own, and he, albeit he knew it not, was called of God, and was yet to undo the Latin bolts and bars, and break in sunder the monastic chains, and give a good honest German liberty to the blessed Word of God, and bring home its hallowed light to thousands of darkened hearths and homes, and to millions of benighted souls. He himself was first to learn from it the fulness of the blessings of the gospel of peace, and then become the foremost Bible teacher of the world.

Soon he was ordained a priest, and then very soon appointed professor of philosophy in the University of Wittemberg. Staupitz recommended him to Frederick, Elector of Saxony, and the Elector sent him his commission. At once besides the duties of his own professorship, he began giving lectures during an unoccupied hour, upon the Bible, first upon the Psalms, then upon Romans. It was a new thing under the sun. His lectures were clear, warm, stirring, eloquent, powerful. His fame spread out. Students gathered in. Soon by appointment of the Elector, and by the persuasion of Staupitz, and by the hand of Carlstadt he was made "Doctor in Theology,"

Biblical doctor, and sworn to defend the gospel with all his strength. Now at last he was in the very chair, and the very work designed for him from the first.

But these are the events of his outward life. The life within is that which concerns us. We have seen how Luther came to the faith of the forgiveness of sins. We will now trace the steps of his final and full freedom of soul through faith in the Lord Jesus. One day, while studying Romans for a lecture to the students, the words of the prophet Habakkuk as quoted by Paul, Rom. 1:17 — "The just shall live by faith," struck their light through his soul. Here was the grand principle of life and righteousness. He saw it, grasped it, exulted in it, and began teaching it with all the force and fire of his eloquence and genius. There were, it is true, applications of this great principle which he was not yet prepared to see, or to make, both to the church and to his own heart and life. But the principle of justification by faith was no longer a hidden one to him, and it infused a new life and a new power into his soul and his teachings. He applied it with sunbeam clearness to the forgiveness of sins. He saw how God could be just, and yet justify him that believeth in Jesus, however great his sins might be. Selected not long after to represent seven convents in matter of difference between them and the Vicar General, at the court of the Roman Pontiff he set off, led by the hand of God into Rome itself, to witness with his own eyes and ears the blasphemous hollowness, and putrid corruptions of the church. On the way he was again taken ill, and again brought to look down into the grave and up to the Judgment Bar of God. His sins troubled him. The old Erfurth horror of darkness returned upon him. But in tine midst of it the words of the prophet, "The just shall live by faith" came again to him with a new force and filled him with the light of heaven. And yet again, while looking upon the ruins of ancient Rome, and almost overwhelmed by the conviction that the Rome which then was would one day be also in ruins, the holy city would pass away, lie in ashes, the same words came to his relief and comfort again, "The just shall live by faith." The church shall live though Rome should die. Christ lives, and the gates of hell shall never prevail against his church. Luther had not yet learned to take the Lord Jesus for his sanctification. He had one process for the forgiveness of sins, that of faith, and another for the pursuit of holiness, that of works. He believed in Jesus, and trusted that for the sake of Jesus who had died, and risen again for his justification, his sins were all freely forgiven. But he longed for a holy heart and a holy life, and sought them by means not by faith. The truth that Jesus is all to the sinner, that in Jesus he has all if he takes him for all, he had not yet perceived. Christ a propitiation he accepted, but Christ a sanctification he rejected. Strange that having Christ, and believing in him, and having in him the fountain of holiness, indeed our own holiness, just as really and fully as he is our own sacrifice for sin, we should go about to work out, or seek for holiness of heart imparted to us from God aside from, not in Christ. Yet so it is. So it was with Luther. At Rome he performed all holy offices, and visited every sacred place, hungering and thirsting after righteousness. One day he sought to secure a special indulgence promised to all holy pilgrims who should climb Pilate's staircase, so called, on their knees. This Pilate's staircase was said to have been transported bodily by miracle, in the night, from Jerusalem to Rome. As Luther crept painfully from stone to stone upward, suddenly he heard, as he thought, a voice of thunder in the depths of his heart, "The just shall live by faith." These words had often before told him that the just are made alive by faith, but now they thundered through his soul the truth that even so "the just shall live (be kept alive) by faith." By faith they shall be kept by the power of God; by faith they shall make progress onward and upward; by faith their sins shall be forgiven; and by faith their hearts and lives shall be made holy.

Ah! well might the historian say of Luther that "this was a creative word for the reformer," now for the first time he was freed from all false processes of salvation, and fully established in the true. Faith now, as the condition, and Jesus as the salvation he saw was the whole. Full salvation was in Jesus, and Jesus was the soul's in full, through full trust in him. When this word resounded in this new force through his soul, it is no wonder that Luther sprang to his feet upon the stone steps up which he had been crawling like a worm, horrified at himself, and struck with shame for the degradation to which superstition had debased him, and fled from the scene of his folly. Luther himself says, "Then l felt myself born again as a new man, and I entered by an open door into the very paradise of God. From that hour l saw the precious and holy Scriptures with new eyes. l went through the whole Bible. l collected a multitude of passages which taught me what the work of God was. Truly this text of St. Paul was to me the very gate of heaven."

Chapter Three - Examples Compared

"YE ARE MY WITNESSES."

The experience of Luther has been given at length because the great reformer stands in forefront of Protestantism, a true and noble type of the real ripe, whole-souled Christian, very much abridged, and condensed, however, from the accounts given by his biographers. It is entitled to great weight as an example. Let not its force be broken by the thought that Luther was great, and a special instrument of God specially endowed. So far as salvation is concerned, Luther stood with us precisely. He was a man, and a sinner, as we all are. Faith in him and in us is the same thing, and Jesus is the same to all and for all in all time. The same rays of the sun of righteousness shining through the same tears of penitence, cause the same bow of the covenant to arch the same clouds of despair, in all ages and nations, and the same eye of faith discerns the promise and rests joyously upon it, in all persons, alike the great and the small.

It will be observed that Luther's first light and comfort was in the forgiveness of sins; and the last and greatest, in the full apprehension of Christ as his sanctification. We shall have occasion to see the same thing in every instance as we go on. How this comes to pass we shall see very clearly when we come to speak of the philosophy of Christian experience.

With some, the force of Luther's example may be broken by the fact that he was bred in all the superstitions of Rome, and had a second shell to break through, after he was out of the first. We will, therefore, take another example: one from the ranks of those bred in the full blaze of the light of the Protestant day, three centuries after Luther's time.

was educated at Geneva, the home of Calvin and the stronghold of the Reformation. Calvin himself is not a better representative of the reformed religion, or a nobler champion than Merle D'Aubigne, the famous historian of the Reformation. His conversion was at Geneva, while in the university. The subsequent deeper work was several years later at Kiel in Germany. His conversion, together with others, a noble band, was by the instrumentality of one of the Lord's Scottish noblemen, Robert Haldane. In some sort it was the payment of an old debt of three hundred years' standing due from Scotland to Geneva. Knox, driven from home by bloody persecutions, found refuge three several times in Geneva, and during the years of his stay there, while, doubtless he imparted much of his iron energy and Scottish firmness; he certainly received much of the clear light of the Swiss mountain height so elevated above the murky mists of the Campagna, the Tiber and Rome. Right eagerly Robert Haldane sought to pay the debt, and God helped him, as the conversion of D'Aubigne, Monod, Gonthier, Gaussin, Rieu, and many more will testify.

Dr. Cheever, as quoted in the memoirs of R. & J. A. Haldane, speaks of D'Aubigne's conviction as follows:

"At this juncture it was that D'Aubigne heard of the visit of Mr. Haldane. He heard of him as the English or Scotch gentleman who spoke so much about the Bible, a thing which seemed very strange to him and the other students to whom the Bible was a shut book. He afterwards met Mr. Haldane at a private house, along with some of his friends, and heard him read from an English Bible, a chapter from the Epistle to the Romans, concerning the natural corruption of man, a doctrine in regard to which he had never received any instruction. He was astonished to hear of men being corrupt by nature, but clearly convinced by the passages read to him, he said to Mr. Haldane, 'Now I do indeed see this doctrine in the Bible.' 'Yes,' replied the good man, 'but do you see it in your heart?' It was but a simple question, but it came home to his conscience. It was the sword of the Spirit; and from that time he saw and felt that his heart was indeed corrupted, and knew from the Word of God that he could be saved by grace alone in Jesus Christ."

The conversion of D'Aubigne was decided, clear and unmistakable. He himself speaks of it in his "Travelling Recollections in Germany, England and Scotland," chap. I, § 2., in these explicit words, "I had been seized by the Word of God;" (while at the university in Geneva;) "I had believed in the divinity of Christ, in original sin, the power of which I had experienced in my own heart; and in justification by faith. I had experienced the joys of the new birth."

Of the later, deeper work he speaks more fully in the same connexion and just as explicitly. After his conversion he completed his course at the university at Geneva, was ordained, went to Germany; pursued study still further, first at Leipsic, then at Berlin, and then spent four years as a pastor over the French church at Hamburg. Several years had thus fled before the time came for the Lord to give him the final full knowledge of Jesus as all in all. It was on this wise. At an inn, in Kiel, he had planned and entered upon a journey with two of his old Genevan fellow students and fellow converts, to Copenhagen. They met at Kiel, a remarkable trio: Rev. Frederick Monod settled at Paris; Rev. Charles Rien, pastor of Fredencia in Jutland; and D'Aubigne. Steamboats were irregular; they waited at the hotel. D'Aubigne was then in the midst of a terrible struggle. Kiel was a university, and Kheuker, an old champion of the word and an experienced Christian; was Biblical professor there. D'Aubigne says, "I called upon him and requested him to elucidate several passages of Scripture for my satisfaction.**** The old doctor would not enter into any detailed solution of my difficulties. 'Were I to succeed in ridding you of them,' he said to me, 'others would soon arise; there is a shorter, deeper, more complete way of annihilating them. Let Christ be really to you the Son of God, the Saviour, the Author of eternal life! Only be firmly settled in his grace, and then these difficulties of detail will never stop you! The light which proceeds from Christ will disperse all your darkness.' The old divine had shown me the way: I saw it was the right one, but to follow it was a hard task."

The Way. Yes, indeed! and the right one. Happy for D'Aubigne that he saw it! Happy that its hardness did not keep him back from it! While they waited at Kiel for the steamboat, they devoted part of the time to reading the Word of God together, a pattern for all detained Christian travellers. Rieu was chaplain. D'Aubigne says of him that he had even then far outstripped both himself and M. Monod in the divine life. Two years after, he finished his brilliant career upon earth by a triumphant transit to heaven. His converse was very sweet. They all three communicated their thoughts to each other on the Word of God, but Rieu brought out the hidden riches of the Book of God most abundantly.

"We were studying the Epistle to the Ephesians," says D'Aubigne, "and had got to the end of the third chapter. When we read the two last verses 'Now unto him who is able to do EXCEEDING ABUNDANTLY above all that we ask or think, according to the power that worketh in us, unto him be glory' &c. This expression fell upon my soul as a revelation from God. 'He can do by his power,' I said to myself, 'above all we ask, above all even that we think, nay, EXCEEDING ABUNDANTLY above all! A full trust in Christ for the work to be done within my poor heart now filled my soul. We all three knelt down, and, although I had never fully confided my inward struggles to my friends, the prayer of Rieu was filled with such admirable faith, as he would have uttered had he known all my wants. When I arose, in that inn-room at Kiel, I felt as if my 'wings were renewed as the wings of eagles.' From that time forward I comprehended that all my own efforts were of no avail; that Christ was able to do all by his 'power that worketh in us;' and the habitual attitude of my soul was to lie at the foot of the cross, crying to Him, 'Here am I, bound hand and foot, unable to move, unable to do the least thing to get away from the enemy who oppresses me. Do all thyself. I know that thou wilt do it. Thou wilt even do exceeding abundantly above all that I ask.'

"I was not disappointed; all my doubts were removed, my anguish quelled, and the Lord 'extended to me peace as a river.' Then I could comprehend with all saints what is the breadth, and length, and depth, and height; and know the love of Christ which passeth knowledge. Then was I able to say, 'Return unto thy rest, O my soul: for the Lord hath dealt bountifully with thee.'"

In these sketches of experience, nothing has been said in either case touching the question of entire instantaneous sanctification, or Christian perfection. Neither the great reformer or the great historian of the Reformation made any profession of perfection themselves. Indeed Luther expressly disclaims it, and D'Aubigne records the disclaimer. Yet in both the soul and marrow of the full experience of salvation at the last, was the perception and the reception of the Lord Jesus as their righteousness in the sense of sanctification, as already before they had taken him as their righteousness in the sense of justification; for these senses are both included in the term "righteousness of God" as used by Paul, and exulted in by Luther, and in both senses Christ is complete to the believer, and in both, the believer is complete in Christ.' Luther and D'Aubigne alike hungered after righteousness, true holiness, and either would fain have satisfied himself with husks from any hand, if he could, but he could not. God had in store for both, the true bread that cometh down from heaven to the full. Both struggled long and manfully, each in his own way, both in vain, until each gave up his own way, and took the Lord Jesus as THE WAY. Both fought resolutely, and were foiled in every onset, and would have fallen at last slain and conquered, had not God taught them the sweet truth uttered by the loving disciple, "This is the victory that overcometh — even your faith." By faith at last, by full trust in Jesus, both conquered an abiding peace, and both gained the full salvation.

To these examples scores upon scores might be added of the same class; those who have given themselves wholly to Jesus, and taken Jesus wholly to themselves, and so found the abiding sunshine, and the serene sky of full salvation, but who yet make no profession of perfection, but like Luther and D'Aubigne, disclaim it. The memoirs of the great and good, gone to their reward, abound in such, and the living witnesses are many. Richard Baxter, Jonathan Edwards, Hewitson, McCheyne, Mrs. Edwards, Adelaide Newton, and a host of others. In the Life and Times of Richard Baxter, 2 vols. 8 vo. London, a very circumstantial account is given of this great man's experience. Quite as distinct as either Luther's or D'Aubigne's, both as to his final full apprehension of Christ as all in all, and as to his conversion years before. President Edwards himself has given to the world a sketch as remarkable as either, known to be the experience of his own beloved consort; one of the happiest Christians that ever lived. And in the details he has spread out of his own inner life, if the moments of the first and the last great transitions are less distinctly traced, the same fulness of faith at the last, and the same precious results are as clearly seen.

The memoirs of Hewitson by Baily, and of Adelaide Newton by the same, furnish each a lovely instance also. Hewitson describes a long and severe struggle years after his Conversion, terminating finally in such an apprehension of Christ in his fulness, as his righteousness — sanctification — as filled him with heavenly consolations, and abode with him ever after.

But we have no space even for references to each of the noble many in this bright cloud of witnesses, much less for their experience in detail. Other classes must be compared with this if we would gain a clear comprehension of the whole subject. We will call this class THE LUTHERAN. Another may be called THE WESLEYAN, and a third THE OBERLINIAN. The Wesleyans received their first light in this matter, and their first impulse from the Moravian brethren of Germany. And the Oberlinians took their terms, and some colors and shades of view from the Wesleyans. Both use the terms, "perfect love," "Christian perfection" "entire sanctification" to describe the experience in question, and "doctrine of sanctification," or "doctrine of holiness," as expressive of their creed about it. The Oberlinians differ from the Wesleyans in their philosophy of the will of man, and of the law of God. Their view of the claims of the law as graduated to the sinners ability, enables them to hold and profess perfect sanctification when they come to yield wholly to the known will of God, and take

Christ wholly as their righteousness and true holiness. The Wesleyans admit the claims of the law of God as requiring absolute perfection, like the spotless purity of Jesus, and the holy angels, and make no professions of it, but only of Christian perfection, making a broad distinction between Christian and angelic perfection.

Both Wesleyans and Oberlinians differ from Lutherans in the use of terms, and in the theology of the experience described, but aside from this, in all that is essential in the experience itself all are agreed. Of the Wesleyans, the memoirs of Carvasso are clearest and simplest in the development of the experimental truth. He was a man of God. His faith was wonderful, and his views clear as the light. Bramwell if less clear was even more absorbed and ardent. Mrs. Rogers was truly seraphic. Mrs. Fletcher's memoirs are very fascinating, as indeed are all these and many more of this class. They have opened the eyes of thousands to the higher walks of Christian life, and impelled tens of thousands to press for the mark. But so far as we can see, there is no essential difference between the experience they describe, and those of Luther and D'Aubigne, Baxter and Edwards. All alike begin with a sense of their guilt, and peril, and come sooner or later to a sense of sins forgiven, blotted out in the blood of Jesus, and then, again sooner or later, in every case, hungering and thirsting for true holiness is induced, and after varied struggles the issue in all alike, is that of finding in Christ the end of the law for sanctification.

This unity will be apparent if we place any two of them side by side. Here for instance are the expressions of Mrs. Rogers, and of D'Aubigne from their own pens in their own words, descriptive of their own views and feelings at the moment their struggles were crowned with the victory that overcometh, viz., full trust in Jesus.

D'AUBIGNE

[Pardon the repetition, it seems to be necessary.]

After describing his conversion clearly, and the subsequent struggles and turn given to the current of his desires and efforts, by the counsels of the good old champion of the faith Kluker at Kiel, and the scene at Inn, with his two fellow travelers, Monod and Rieu; their reading in the word of God, the III of Ephesians, and the power with which the two last verses were set home to his heart, says, "When I arose, in that inn-room at Kiel, I felt as if my 'wings were renewed as the wings of eagles.' From that time forward, I comprehended that my own efforts were of no avail; that Christ was to do all by his 'power that worketh in us,' and the habitual attitude of my soul was to lie at the foot of the cross, crying to Him, 'Here am I, bound hand and foot, unable to move, unable to do the least thing to get away from the enemy that oppresses me. Do all thyself. I know that thou wilt; thou wilt even do exceeding abundantly above all that I ask.'

I was not disappointed, all my doubts were soon dispelled, and not only was I delivered from the inward anguish which in the end would have destroyed me, had not God been faithful; but the Lord 'extended peace to me like a river.' Then I could 'comprehend with all saints what is the breadth, and length, and depth, and height, and know the love of Christ which passeth knowledge,'" (filled with all the fullness of God.)

MRS. ROGERS

After all the record of her earlier contest, and earlier experience of sins forgiven, and after describing her heart-searchings, doubts, fears, desires, and efforts for true holiness, comes at last to the moment when she sees Christ to be all in all, and receives him. Then she says, "Lord, my soul is delivered of her burden. I am emptied of all. I am at thy feet, a helpless, worthless worm; but take hold of thee as my fullness! Everything that I want, thou art. Thou art wisdom, strength, love, holiness: yes, and thou art mine! I am conquered and subdued by love. Thy love sinks me into nothing; it overflows my soul. O, my Jesus, thou art all in all! In thee I behold and feel all the fullness of the Godhead mine. I am now one with God; the intercourse is open; sin, inbred sin, no longer hinders the close communion, and God is all my own. O, the depths of that solid peace my soul now felt!"

And this, like D'Aubigne she describes, not merely as the rapture of a favored hour, but as the habitual attitude of the soul, at the foot of the cross.

"Yea, Christ all in all to me
And all my heart is love."

"With every coming hour
I prove
His nature and his name is Love."

Like David in his expressions of love to Jonathan when these dear friends parted in the field, Mrs. Rogers "excelled" in ardency of feelings and words, but in all that is essential there is not a single line of difference. Both are self-emptied, both prostrate in the dust at the foot of the cross; both accept Jesus as all in all, and find themselves conquerors, and more than conquerors through faith in his name.

Chapter Four - Explanations

THE FACTS AND THE PHILOSOPHY OF THE FACTS.

"WISDOM IS JUSTIFIED OF ALL HER CHILDREN."

In these sketches and references the first and great fact is that of full salvation through full trust in Jesus. This fact needs no proof. It is at once the provision and the demand of the gospel, and is of course the privilege and duty of all. The Apostle Paul lived in it himself, and commended it, and commanded it, to others. The apostles and primitive Christians generally enjoyed it from the day of Pentecost onward. There were exceptions certainly. The Galatians seem to have been turned aside from the fulness and simplicity of the faith. Having begun in the spirit, they thought to be made perfect by works, and the apostle wrote them with all plainness and urgency of speech, to induce them to look to Christ and Christ alone for holiness, telling them that he travailed in birth for them again, until Christ should formed in them the hope of glory. And there were other churches beside those of Galatia where, through the blindness of unbelief, they failed of the fulness of God. But, as a general thing, we hear only of the same life of faith in its fulness, and fulness of joy in all, until after the death of all the apostles, save John, and he exiled from the churches and shut up in the lone Isle of Patmos. Then, when the apostles were gone, and the days of miracles were ended, and inspired teaching ceased in the churches, and Satan began to be loosed — then, in the epistles of him who walks in glory amidst the golden candlesticks, we have the first intimation that the light of the candles was beginning to grow dim.

And surely Luther and Baxter, Wesley and D'Aubigne, full and rich as their experience of grace and salvation was, had not outstripped Peter and John, Paul and Apollos! Neither have the Lutherans, as we have named them, or the Wesleyans, or Oberlinians, got beyond primitive Christians! Nay, if we shall carry the comparison back to the bright cloud of witnesses, who passed off before Christ's coming upon earth, as they are called up in array before us in the beautiful citation by the apostle in the eleventh of Hebrews, we shall hardly find the brightest of moderns outstripping these worthies of old, either in fulness of faith, or fulness of salvation. Going about, therefore, to prove that there is such an experience would be but a fool's work! If any one doubts, with the Bible in his hand, surely the rushlight of any other proof in the face of this noon-day blaze, would go for nothing!

Neither does this fact need explanation any more than it needs proof. It is simply the result of the gospel received in its fulness. Christ is set forth as all in all for the sinner's salvation, and the sinner who receives him as such, and abides in him, has full salvation. But there is another fact which should be explained: the fact that in the instances given, as in others not referred to, there is a second experience, distinct from the first — sometimes years after the first — and as distinctly marked, both as to time and circumstances and character, as the first — a second conversion, as it is often called. Baxter speaks of this in his case as quite as important as the first. So does James Brain and Taylor, and many others also; while in such cases as Luther's and D'Aubigne's, both the experience and its importance are so marked as to speak for themselves. Some have tried to account for this fact by denying the reality of the first experience. "These people were deceived," say they, "and not converted at all, as they suppose, in the first instance."

But if Luther was not converted, who then is? If D'Aubigne was deceived in the first instance, who then is not? If to have been convinced of the deep depravity of the heart by nature, and led to accept Jesus as the Son of God and Saviour of sinners, and to have experienced the joys of the new birth, is not to have been really converted, but deceived, tell us then what conversion is? No, no; this supposition does violence to truth and common sense; it will not do. We must have a better solution, or none.

Others have thought to solve the problem by calling the second experience simply a return from backsliding. But in each of the cases given, we have the testimony of the witnesses themselves, that it was more than this, a deeper work of grace, a fuller apprehension of Christ, a more complete and abiding union with him than at the first. The witnesses themselves being judges in their own case, this solution is not the true one. We must go deeper for it. Thousands in every age since the primitive, have backslidden and returned again without any such great and permanent advancement in the divine life, as that set forth in the examples before us. In Luther's experience, as he describes it, there was that which made the Bible a new book to him. Already, in his conversion a key had been put into his hand to unlock vast treasures of truth in the Word of God, but it was only after his final and full apprehension of Christ as his sanctification, superadded to his knowledge of Christ in the forgiveness of sins, that the abundance and wealth of the Bible became the Reformer's. And D'Aubigne tells us that after that scene in the inn-room at Kiel he went through and through the Bible anew, gathering up innumerable passages full of new significance to him. His description recalls another very like it, under like circumstances. One who had but just then passed through a similar "second conversion," compared himself to a child sent on an errand, but finding by the wayside so many beautiful flowers and luscious fruits, now on this side, now on that, inviting the hand to pluck them, as to keep the child busy all day long, forgetful of the errand. "So," said he, "has it happened to me with my Bible. I have set out to find some desired passage, and so many things beautiful and new have caught my eye in passing along, as to tempt me to dally, and pick, and eat, and drink in their sweet fragrance all the day long, forgetful of my errand. And then too," he went on to say "when I kneel down to pray, praise only swells my heart, for all the glorious things of Christ." Ah, there is vastly more in such an experience, than mere return from backsliding! Then, too, above and beyond all this, it is never the returning backslider who comes into the fulness of this experience. Indeed, if backsliding and returning would really bring men into this gospel fulness, pity but the whole church would backslide and return. It would be a grand thing for the cause of Christ, and for their own comfort and joy. But in point of fact, in every case, if the reader will examine, it will be seen that it is only the earnest and the active Christian, the working, struggling one, who comes to the knowledge of Christ in his fulness. The backslider returns only to the point attained when he turned back at most, and hard struggling for that! But the work in question is a higher height, and a deeper depth, in the comprehension both of the love of Christ which passeth knowledge, and of the way of salvation by faith.

Neither of these solutions is the true one. The true, however, is not difficult. Mark it well: It is in perfect harmony with all religious experience. What we call experimental religion, is simply this: The sinner is first awakened to a realization of his guilt before God, and of his danger, it may be too. He really feels, that is, he experiences his, need of salvation, and becomes anxious and eager to do anything to secure it. Tries perhaps all sorts of expedients, except the one only and true, in vain. Then at last his eyes are opened to see that Jesus Christ is set forth to be his salvation, and that all he has to do, just as he is, without one grain of purity or merit, in all his guilt and pollution, to trust in his Saviour, and now he sees and feels, that is, he experiences, that Jesus Christ is the Way, the Truth, and the Life, the very Saviour he needs. In Jesus he triumphs and exults. In Jesus he revels and rejoices. Jesus is the one amongst ten thousands, altogether lovely. The only one in heaven or on earth to be desired, filling all the orbit of his soul with faith, and hope and love. This in substance is the sum of all religious experience. All may be condensed into three words: the first expressive of the sinner's necessities — SALVATION: the second expressive of the gospel provision for the sinner, a SAVIOUR; and the third embodying the condition of the sinner's entire deliverance, FAITH.

And now to account for the two distinct experiences, each so marked and important, and so alike in character, we have only to consider two facts, viz., first, that the sinner's necessities are two-fold and distinct, although both are included in the one word salvation. We express the two in the words of that favorite hymn, Rock of Ages, when we sing,

> "*Be of sin the double cure,*
> "*Save from wrath and make me pure.*"

And the Psalmist makes the distinction in the second verse of the thirty-second Psalm, saying, "Blessed is the man to whom the Lord imputeth not iniquity; and in whose spirit there is no guile."

The apostle Paul generally includes both in the one term "Righteousness of God," as "to all and upon all that believe," but in the thirtieth verse of the first chapter of first Corinthians, he separates them and marks them by the distinct terms, "righteousness," and "sanctification," and now of late the whole Christian world, has come to distinguish them by the now limited and definite terms, justification and sanctification. Luther used the term justification as including both; in the same way that the apostle Paul used the expression righteousness of God. Justification in the great Reformer's sense, was being made righteous; that is, being reckoned righteous before God, and 'being made righteous in heart and life. Nevertheless the two things are distinct and different in their nature, and are expressive of two great and equal wants of the sinner. He must be just in the eye of the law, justified before God. And he must also be holy in heart and life, or he cannot be saved.

This is the first fact to be taken into account in coming to an understanding of the two separate and distinct experiences, so clearly marked in such cases as Luther's, and D'Aubigne's. Another is that, practically always perhaps, and theologically often, we separate between the two in our views and efforts, to secure them to ourselves, until we are experimentally taught better. We have one process for acceptance with God, that is faith; and another for progress in holiness, that is works. After having found acceptance in Jesus by faith, we think to go on to perfection by strugglings and resolves, by fastings and prayers, not knowing the better way of taking Christ for our sanctification, just as we have already taken him for our justification. We see and believe in Jesus as our atonement on earth, and our Advocate and Mediator in heaven, but we fail to see and receive him as our ever-present Saviour from sin now here with us in the hourly scenes of the daily journey heavenward. The consequence is, that as in the first instance we tried all sorts of expedients, except the right one, and failed in every one, until at last the Lord opened our eyes to see both our own folly in all these vain attempts, and at the same breath to see the wisdom of God in giving us His Son our Saviour as the Way; even so now again in the second, we try all, and all in vain, until again in this new and equal necessity, we find anew that all our ways are vain, and that Jesus is the Way.

These two facts will account for these cases of "second conversion." Let it not be supposed, however, that in every instance there must be two distinct experiences, separated by a gulph of vain strugglings. It is not necessary that there should be one even. Let Jesus be received as the all in all, and that is enough! Whoever can say, "Jesus is mine and I am his, that he is complete and I am complete in him," and say the truth, has the experience whether he has an experience to relate, or not. He has the Rock of Ages for his foundation, and all the driving storms, and beating tempests, and swelling floods of time and eternity, will not sweep it from under him. Christ, without any marked experience whatever, is all-sufficient; but the most brilliant experience without Christ, would be only quick-sand in the day of trial. Loyola"s experience was as brilliant as Paul's; and Mahomet's was even more wonderful than either; just as some counterfeits are really finer in appearance than the genuine; but that did not make the great Jesuit a saint, except in his own eyes, and in the Romish calendar, nor the false prophet an angel anywhere outside of his own sensual paradise.

Some voyagers heavenward trouble themselves all the live-long voyage, clear to the very entrance of the haven of rest, with doubts whether after all they have really set sail at all or not, because they had not the same struggles and difficulties in hoisting anchor and getting the canvas spread to the breezes of heaven, that others describe! Surely it should be enough that they are on shipboard, with anchor up, sails set, steam working, outward bound, plowing the deep at the rate of fifteen knots an hour! What if they did set out in the nighttime, or in a fog? Is it not enough that the captain and the pilot knew how to find the way, and that they are now out in the sunlight, on the open sea, and bounding over the billows to the desired haven?

This, by the way. It is certainly pleasant to have distinct recollections of one's conversion, and also of the moment and the circumstances when full trust for full salvation was first reposed in Jesus, but this is by no means indispensable. To be in the way, to have Jesus for the all in all, is the great thing.

There remains yet one thing more to be done before closing these explanations. In the preceding examples and comparisons, certain differences were shown between the three classes, which, for convenience, we named Lutherans, Wesleyans, and Oberlinians. It will be important to note again, first the points, both of agreement and of difference between them, and then to give the reasons of both their differences and their agreements.

It is worthy .of special note again that their differences are altogether those of opinion, not at all of fact. All are agreed as to the essential facts of the experience in question. The shades of difference in the manner of narrating are not at all essential. All agree especially in the one great matter, that the experience is that of the way of sanctification by faith: that of really practically receiving Jesus for sanctification by faith, as before he had been received as the sacrifice for sins. This may be variously expressed, but this is the marrow and substance of the whole matter in every case and with every class.

Again: all agree as to the fact that this practical, experimental apprehension of Christ is instantaneous in every case, whether the instant can be marked, as in the cases referred to, or not. However long the struggles beforehand, and however gradual the rising of the light afterwards in the soul, there is a moment when Christ is first seen to be The Way, and when the soul leaves every other way and trusts solely in Jesus. In these facts all agree. And it may be added, that in the one essential doctrine of the way of sanctification, as by faith and not by works, they all agree, of course, if they agree in its practical reception in the experience in question. Theologically, therefore, they are so far in harmony.

Now the differences are, first, as to whether this experience is that of entire instantaneous sanctification or not. Whether the instant the sinner is given up to Christ to be "Sanctified soul, body and spirit, and preserved blameless, until the coming of our Lord," as the apostle prays that the Thessalonians may be, whether then the sinner is indeed, in that moment, made perfect in holiness or not. Or if not, whether in any proper sense he may be spoken of as perfect.

Oberlinians affirm, in the case, absolute moral perfection.
Wesleyans affirm a modified perfection called "Christian."

Lutherans affirm neither, but deny both. Then as to terms descriptive of the experience there is a corresponding difference.

Oberlinians use freely and without qualification the term "entire sanctification."

Wesleyans also, use the word entire, in a restricted sense, though their favorite names are "Perfect love" and "Christian perfection," as modifying, and qualifying the idea of absolute perfection.

Lutherans have discussed the experience less as a thing distinct, and therefore have known it less, and named it less distinctively, than either Wesleyans or Oberlinians.

Cases of it have always occurred in every great awakening, and often also in solitary instances, in the furnace of affliction or under the special influences of sovereign grace and power. Such cases have generally received the convenient name, "second conversion:" but in the standards, as in the Westminster Assembly's Confession, it is called, "The full assurance of grace and salvation," and elsewhere, "The full assurance of faith," while in hymns it is often named, "Full salvation."

Now as to the reasons of these agreements and these differences, it will be easy to see them, if we scan the matter closely.

All agree in the facts of the experience, because the facts themselves are in harmony in all cases. And all agree in the doctrine of sanctification by faith, because in every case, that is the great principle received experimentally in place of sanctification by works. And all agree that this experimental reception of Christ for sanctification is instantaneous, because it could not be otherwise. For in every change of one principle of action for another, however long the matter may be under consideration before hand, the change at last when it does occur, must from the nature of the case be instantaneous.

But while all agree in this, and thus far — just here the separation begins.

Oberlinians look upon the soul's sanctification as complete, entire, wanting nothing, the instant Christ is accepted for entire sanctification.

Lutherans look upon this, the acceptance of Christ as the soul's sanctification, as the entrance merely upon the true and only way of being made holy, as the first full discovery of the real and the right way.

Wesleyans take a middle view, indefinite, and therefore undefinable. They do not believe in the absolutely perfected holiness of the soul the instant it trusts fully in Jesus for holiness of heart. They freely admit that imperfections may and do still exist, while yet a sort of modified perfection is attained, as they think.

Now what is the right and the truth of the matter? Exactly what is attained in this experience?

Christ. Christ in all his fulness. Christ as all in all. Christ objectively and subjectively received and trusted in. That is all. And that is enough.

But what as to holiness of heart? Nothing! Nothing but a sense of self-emptiness and vileness, and helplessness. Nothing but a sense of unholiness, and a full consciousness that all efforts and resolutions, and strugglings and cries for holiness of heart, are just as vain as the attempts of a leopard or an Ethiopian to bathe white in any waters. This with a sense of absolute dependence upon Christ for holiness of heart and life, just as for the forgiveness of sin is the sum and substance of the soul's attainment. At the same time while this deep self-abasement, and utter self-abhorrence fills the soul, there is on the other hand just as deep a sense of the all-sufficiency and perfect loveliness of Christ, and a realization of the fulness of his love, and an assurance of his ability to do exceeding abundantly above all that we can ask Or think, according to the power that worketh in us. And a confidence that he will do it, according to the plan of God.

Then what follows?

Then follows the work according to our faith.

By faith the soul is now placed in the hands of Christ, as the clay in the hands of the potter; and by faith, Christ is received by the soul as the potter to mold it at his own sovereign will, into a vessel for the Master's own use and for the King's own table.

By faith the soul now is opened as a mirror to the Master, and as in a crystal fount of unrippled face, the Master's image is taken in all its meekness and majesty.

By faith the soul is put into the hands of Christ, like paper into the hands of the printer to be unfolded and softened and printed, with all the glorious things of God. And by faith Christ is taken to the soul like an unopened book, title page read it may be, and portrait frontispiece scanned and admired, but its leaves uncut, and its treasures of wisdom and knowledge all unexplored, all in reserve, to be gained by daily and hourly reading, in all after time.

By the power of God, in the light of truth, a new starting point has been gained. A new and higher level has been reached, and in the new light all things take on a new loveliness, and from the new starting point the race becomes swifter and yet easier. A starting point it is however, and not the goal reached, or the mark of the prize won. Let this be specially noted, and kept ever in mind. This being the case it is easy to see why the Lutherans should reject the terms and ideas of perfection, as attained in this experience, for it is the beginning, not the end; only the entrance, fully and consciously, by the right principle, upon the process of sanctification — not sanctification completed.

When a man sick unto death, has become fully convinced of the utter hopelessness of his case in his own hands, and thrown away every remedy devised by himself, or recommended by his friends, and sent for a physician who has wisdom to understand and skill to heal his disease, it would be folly to say that at the moment his case was en-trusted to the physician, his cure was complete. So in the Lutheran view, the transfer and the trust of the soul, for the whole work of sanctification by the Holy Spirit is but the first effectual step in the work. It is the door of the way fairly entered, and the way clearly perceived. So much, no more. The goal and the crown are yonder in the glorious future, and in the open vision and unveiled presence of the King immortal and eternal — but as yet invisible — the only wise God our Saviour.

And it is also easy to see why the Wesleyans reject the idea of absolute perfection attained in the experience, for they see and know that, according to their standard of sinless obedience, it is not true. While at the same time it is easy to see how the fact that it is an experimental apprehension of the true way of sanctification, together with the desire to give the experience a distinctive name has led to the adoption of such terms as " Christian perfection" and "Perfect love" with a disclaimer of any profession of sinless perfection or absolute angelic holiness of heart and life.

For the Oberlinian idea that the experience brings the soul into a state of sinless perfection, or entire sanctification the grounds must be sought in three things: first, their philosophy of the will, according to which each volition or choice is in itself absolutely holy, or absolutely unholy and altogether so. So that when God is chosen, while that choice is predominant, the soul is perfectly holy; and when the world is chosen, then while that choice is uppermost, then the soul is perfectly sinful: — This, with their view of the law of God as graduated to the sinner's condition, whatever it is, not requiring of all alike the same entire conformity to the absolute and unchangeable standard of heavenly holiness, but claiming no more than the sinner's earthly blindness permits him to see, and no more than his earthly weakness permits him to do. And to these two a third must be added; viz., their definition of sanctification, according to which it is consecration only — or setting apart to God — and so is man's own work, instead of God's. Whereas, according to the popular acceptation, sanctification is the work of God in the soul after it is set apart to God by voluntary consecration: — These three things taken together, and taken together with the experience, may serve to show us why and how the Oberlinians adopt the terms, and accept the idea of "entire sanctification" as attained in the experience.

As a closing remark: Let it be borne in mind that these differences, are only differences of opinion. Important certainly; but after all, nothing in comparison with the great facts in which all are agreed. Not for a moment should they be allowed to keep one back from securing the great and blessed realities of such an experimental apprehension of Christ and salvation as is set forth in the examples given. The experience is a reality. Jesus is freely offered as our sanctification as well as our justification. Faith — full trust in him will bring full salvation with him to the soul. Let no one fail of the grace of God. "Behold, saith he that openeth and no man shutteth, and shutteth and no man openeth, I have set before thee an open door, and no man can shut it."

Chapter Five - A Stumbling Stone

"GATHER OUT THE STONES." — Isaiah lxii: 11.

When a ponderous train of cars is under way, rushing, roaring, thundering along at the rate of thirty miles an hour, it may indeed be thrown from the track by a trifling thing, a block or a stone, and dashed to atoms; but it can be brought safely to a stand-still only by reversing the engine and applying all the power of the brakes. But when standing all still, silent, motionless, a mere pebble before a single wheel will defy all the mighty force of the locomotive to move the train a hair. Just so when fully convinced of the reality and value of the experience exemplified, and fairly on the stretch for it, though there is danger even then of being switched track, or thrown from it by some malicious obstruction placed in the way by our wily adversary; yet no light matter could stop the earnest inquirer from the successful pursuit of the great object in view. Not so, however, in the outset. Then a mere trifle, a misapprehension, a doubt, a fear, a name, one word, may be the pebble on the track, and prevent a single step being taken.

"Perfectionism!" This one word, perfectionism, has kept and is now keeping thousands from examining into the matter at all. It is high time this stumbling stone was gathered out of the way. It may indeed become a beacon light to show the mariner in his heavenward voyage the hidden rock where noble souls have struck in days gone by, and so warn him of its peril, and induce him to give it a wide berth as he passes safely on — but it has no place by right in the way. There is not the least necessary connection between the experience described and perfectionism. It is true that some have connected the two things, but they are entirely distinct and widely different from each other. The experience is a fact, and as a fact it has been exemplified in the instances we have referred to, and thousands besides, in which the theory of perfectionism had not so much as a thought given to it, or if a thought or a word, it was a word of denial, as in the cases of Luther and D'Aubigne. Perfectionism on the other hand is a theory — a notion or system of notions — which may have place in the head, either with or without the experience in the heart. Doubtless there have been many who have accepted the theory of perfectionism, and also come into the experience of full salvation by faith — but there are many also who have taken up the idea of perfectionism, and hell it strenuously without having come into the experience at all. The two things, therefore, have no necessary connection whatever, or the examples given, must go for nothing.

Two illustrations may serve to make this entirely clear. In a little book, which at the time excited some attention and induced an answer from the late venerable Leonard Woods, D. D.," Mahan on Christian Perfection," the author, in a narrative near the close of the book very naively informs us, that first at Oberlin, at a time when there was deep and increasing religious interest, he himself and Mr. Finney, became deeply impressed with the necessity of greater holiness of heart, and after a period of intense anxiety and earnest struggling, first one, then the other came out into the light, to see that the Lord Jesus Christ must be, and was their sanctification, as already they had before received him as their justification.

They began then to preach the full gospel as they then for the first apprehended it. Power attended the preaching. Many were impressed in like manner, and many in like manner came into the light of this second conversion. So the matter went on for six months, while as yet there was no adoption of either the theory or the name of perfectionism. Six whole months it was a nameless experience, or at most called second conversion. After a while, hike the Israelites in the wilderness, when the bread of heaven was given them in the dew of the morning, they began to say one to another, "Manna? manna? What is it? What is it?" Then, as the author informs us, there was quite a shock given them — a thrill of revolt, when one asked in one of their meetings, "Is this Christian perfection?" They hushed the question — but tagged it. A thousand pities that they had not dropped it! But no. By and by, when college vacation came, they two, Mr. M. and Mr. F. took the question to New York with them — as yet three months after the experience received — an open question to be discussed and decided. While in New York, after long deliberation, they accepted and adopted the name Christian perfection, or entire sanctification, and elaborated their own peculiar theory according to their own peculiar philosophy and theology; and with this returned to Oberlin to make it the head quarters and stronghold of the system we have named the Oberlinian.

Now this fact proves one thing beyond the possibility of successful controversy, viz: that in their own case, the experience they described and the theory they imbibed are and were separate and distinct, having no necessary connection whatever with each other.

Another, a very different case, will serve to make separation wider and plainer still. One, who in these pages shall be nameless, though known to the writer, became deeply interested in the subject from reading the memoirs of eminent Christians, James Brainerd Taylor, first of all. By and by he came to associate the terms of the Wesleyans and the ideas of the Oberlinians, with the experience narrated by Taylor. At first it was a hard matter for him to gain his own consent to accept these terms and ideas, and still harder to be willing to acknowledge it. But he did it. The experience he believed to be true, and saw to be excellent. His heart yearned for it. He was not satisfied with what he felt in himself and saw in others. He was sure there was something better within hopeful reach in the gospel. And, alas for him, perfectionism was thrown square in his way. He must accept it and acknowledge it — so he verily thought — or fail of the blessedness he saw in prospect and longed to enjoy.

As God in mercy would have it, this obstacle did not stop him as it has stopped thousands — stopped them, to use a paradox — before they had started. He urged his way onward. The struggle was long and severe. His was the blessedness at last, however, to overcome. He conquered. He fought his way to the tree of life in the midst of the paradise of God, and gained the hidden manna, and the white stone with the new name, known only to himself. But now came instantly an entire change of view about the whole matter of perfection. In the experience, his own utter vileness was shown him, just as Isaiah saw his in the vision of the Lord on his throne; and like Daniel in his vision of the glorious Redeemer in his amber purity and sunlight holiness, he felt his very comeliness turned in-to corruption. While at the same time he saw the fulness of God's glorious grace, and felt that Jesus would be with him evermore, to keep him and work in him by the Holy Spirit his own holy will. And then came instantly the question, " Is this the perfection I have been seeking?" The answer was irresistibly "No." He had been seeking and expecting to be wholly sanctified in a moment by Divine power, and made fully conscious that he was absolutely and entirely holy. But, instead of that, he had his eyes opened to see his utter unholiness and to see that Christ must answer wholly for him, and clothe him altogether with his own (Christ's own) righteousness, and keep him by his own mighty power through faith, and change him as by the spirit of the Lord from glory to glory into his own image. He rose therefore from his knees, not to profess himself perfect, by any means, but to say and to feel that Christ was all in all to him, while he was nothing but sin in- himself.

At once and forever he dropped the theory of perfectionism, and the terms, also, as misnomers of the experience, while from that at day on-ward until now he has rejoiced in full salvation, through full trust in Jesus.

Here then we have two illustrations that the theory of perfection, and the fact of the experience in question have no necessary connection. In the first, the experience was gained first while the theory was unthought of, and indeed shocking at the time, and adopted only after months of delay and speculation.

And in the second, the theory was adopted first, months before the experience was gained, and then thrown aside as at variance with the experience in the moment when that was gained.

Another and still different illustration may not be without use.

This whole subject, experience and theory together had been forced upon the attention of one who had been then three years or more a cheerful, decided, happy Christian. It was disagreeable to her, not because she was not anxious to gain all that such an one as she might reasonably hope for. Already she had found more in religion, than in all the round of the gay world most fully tried, and really enjoyed by her. The nectar of love sipped from the lily of the valley, and from the rose of Sharon, had been too sweet to her to be turned from with disgust, or disrelish even. But heresy! the fear of heresy! or of fanaticism, or extravagance! She shrank from the approach of anything threatening in the least to drive her into ultraism. She could not bear the thought of separating between herself and the Christian world, in which she had found such sweet and happy fellowship. Every book upon this subject was avoided. All conversation about it carefully eschewed. At last however, in a leisure, and yet a sacred hour, one Sabbath morning, when kept from the house of prayer by slight illness, her eye fell upon the story of another's experience of this second conversion, or as he called it, Christian perfection. The narrative was simple, sincere, and truthful. She saw it to be true and real, and she saw it to be as blessed as true, and as necessary as blessed. In that hour her resolution was taken. She gave up her fears. Resolved nobly to take the truth, and take with it whatever of loss or cross it might bring. The struggle was severe but short. The Lord graciously led her to believe in Jesus most fully, and she found rest. Peace as a river, joy in its sweet fulness, love inexpressible flowed in from Christ the fountain, and she was beyond measure happy. Her conversion had been bright, hut not brighter than this her second conversion. At once the desire that all might know of this the Christian's precious privilege, rose like the waters of a spring newly opened, filling her heart to the brim, and ready to overflow. She sought opportunity to make the matter known. But now arose a practical difficulty. What should she say she had experienced? A few friends were to meet socially, a parlor gathering, to talk by the way, of what the Lord had done for them in bringing them hitherto in their pilgrimage. She became perplexed, really distressed with the question, "what shall I tell them?" "Shall I tell them I have experienced entire sanctification? I never felt my unholiness more or so much. Shall I say I have been made perfect? That would indeed prove me perverse, for I never saw my imperfection so clearly, or felt it so deeply. I see Christ a perfect Saviour, and he is mine, and all I want; but I am a perfect sinner, needing a perfect Saviour indeed. I cannot say I am perfect. What then shall I say? For I must witness for Jesus. I must try and get others to trust fully in him."

In her perplexity she appealed for advice to a friend, who wisely counselled her that she had nothing at all to do with the question of perfection, least of all to profess herself to be perfect. She had only to tell what a sinner she herself was, and what a Saviour she had found.

This gave her relief at once and forever And although now for many years she has been a constant, faithful, earnest, successful witness for Jesus, testifying the things, and none other than the things he has done for her, she has never felt herself under any necessity to profess Christian perfection, nor yet has she felt her joys and comforts, or her usefulness one jot the less for steering clear of that profession, but greater. She has the liberty as well as the fulness of the blessings of the gospel.

The purpose of these illustrations is not controversy, with those who hold the Oberlinian or the Wesleyan views of this matter, but simply to take up a stumbling stone out of the way of the many thousands in Christendom, who are deterred by it from gaining the higher heights, and deeper depths of the knowledge and love of Jesus, as a Saviour from sin. If it were not for this, the question of perfectionism might sleep forever, without one word of awakening from the writer. And now his object will be fully gained, if in these brief remarks and few illustrations, the fact shall be clearly and fully made known, that none need fear the necessity running into perfectionism, in pressing for all fulness of the riches of the grace of God.

Chapter Six - Not For Me? Why Not?

"FOR THE PROMISE IS UNTO YOU, AND TO YOUR CHILDREN, AND TO ALL THAT ARE AFAR OFF, EVEN AS MANY AS THE LORD OUR GOD SHALL CALL."

Peter at Pentecost concerning the baptism of the Holy Ghost.

Modesty is lovely, presumption is folly, and pride is madness, but there is a holy boldness which is one of the chiefest of the beauties of holiness.

When the apostles were most supported and engrossed by divine influence, made the very temples of the Holy Spirit, and illumined in every chamber of the soul, then they were boldest, and then their adversaries took note of them that they had been with Jesus.

It becomes even Princes and Kings to take the shoes from their feet in their approaches to God, even when called into his presence by the voice of the Lord himself. It is holy ground, and all self-complacency will certainly give place to a deep sense of pollution in the vision of the spotless majesty of the Most High, and strength itself will wilt into weakness in view of his omnipotence. A Job will exclaim, "I abhor myself." An Isaiah will cry, "Woe is me, I am undone!" A Daniel will feel his "comeliness turned into corruption." A John will fall upon his face as a dead man. No strength will remain in him.

And yet when even a child hears his name called, like the little boy in the Tabernacle lent to the Lord forever by his mother — "Samuel! Samuel!" Then it is surely more pleasing to God to have the willing response, "Here Lord am I," than the reluctant plea, "Not me, Lord, not me! send by whom thou wilt send, but not me."

The Lord was offended with Moses for his pertinacious modesty when called and bidden to strike for the liberty of Israel from Egyptian bondage. And also with Barak when sent for by Deborah the prophetess, and commissioned to break the iron yoke of Amalek. And in both cases he divided the responsibility, as they desired, and the glory too! In the one instance making Aaron a large sharer with his brother Moses, and in the other giving one part to Deborah, and another to Jael the wife of Heber the Kenite, leaving only the third to the shrinking Barak.

God is not well pleased with this shrinking plea of the over modest disciple who says, "Not for me." He has opened the new and living way by the blood of the covenant through the rent vail into the most holy place, and exhorts us in the language of the apostle, "Let us enter in boldly." And it is not modesty but unbelief which puts in this shrinking plea.

"Not for me?" Why not? Why, this is the very plea that the unconverted in their utter unbelief of the freeness of God's grace and mercy urge when dressed to fly to Christ for salvation — "Not for me." And yet we who have tasted and felt the love of the Lord know how foolish their plea is. We know that the invitation is unto "all the ends of the earth," and to "Whosoever will." And surely salvation is no more free in the first draught of the waters of Life, than in the second and. deeper. Christ is no more freely offered in the faith of his atonement, than in the assurance of his personal presence and sanctifying power! He has not given himself to us in half of his offices freely, then to withhold himself from us in the other half. If we are content to take him as a half-way Saviour — a deliverer from condemnation, merely, but refuse to look to him as a present Saviour from sin, it is our own fault. He is a full Saviour. And to all who trust him he gives full salvation. To all and to each.

"But this is not like conversion," says an objector. "It is a special matter designed and bestowed upon special instruments of God called to special responsibilities. Luther was a great man, called of God for a great work. Baxter also — Wesley and D'Aubigne. And these great men were endowed with, great faith. I am not like one of these. It would be presumption in me to expect any such measure of faith."

To answer, and silence this plea is very easy — but to do away with the unbelief that utters it is another matter. How do you know, beloved disciple of Jesus, that the Lord is not calling you to be a special instrument specially endowed for great and good things? Has God revealed to you his plans? Can you say certainly that God has not great things in store for you? Luther, a poor monk, buried up in a convent, without a dollar in the world, or a friend to lean upon, or so much as a Bible of his own to read, might have taken up your plea perhaps with quite as much show of reason as you — and yet suppose he had? and had persisted in it, and refused to press for the fulness of salvation? Ah! then he might have remained a monk forever, and the honor and glory of the Reformer would have crowned other instruments. So with you. You may shut yourself out from great light and love and usefulness — you may let another take your crown — but it will be your own fault, through an evil heart of unbelief if you do. And tell me now — upon your own admission, that this second version is a power of distinguished usefulness to who secures it, are you not taking too much yourself in rejecting it? Certainly it does make useful as well as happy Christians, and refusing to for it is no slight matter. You had better weigh it well.

WILLIAM CARVOSSO

was left an orphan at ten, and bound 'prentice to a farmer. His father was a sailor, impressed and compelled to serve on a British man-of-war, and his days were ended at last in the Greenwich Hospital. His mother gave him some instruction in the — to him — difficult art of reading, when a child, but of writing he knew nothing until he was sixty-five years old. In his youth he was inducted into the mysteries of cock-fighting, wrestling, card-playing, and other like things.

At twenty-one years of age it pleased God to arrest him and bring him to Christ. His sister, just then newly converted, was the means of this. His struggles were great. Satan tempted him, tried him. It was hard to give up the world. Unbelief whispered, "The day of grace is passed: it is now too late." But at last he came to the determination, "Whether saved or lost, never to cease crying for mercy." "And the moment this resolution was formed in my heart," he says, "Christ appeared within, and God pardoned all my sins, and set my soul at liberty. The Spirit himself now bore witness with my spirit that I was a child of God."

This was his conversion. For a time all was fair, peaceful, joyous, happy. By and by, however, he discovered a deeper depth of his necessities. In his own graphic simile,"My heart appeared to me as a small garden with a large stump in it, which had been recently cut down level with the ground, and a little loose earth strewed over it. Seeing something shooting up I did not like, on attempting to pluck it up, I discovered the deadly remains of the carnal mind, and what a work must be done before I could be meet for the inheritance of the saints in light.' What I now wanted was inward holiness."

One night about a year after his conversion, he returned from a meeting greatly distressed with a sense of his unholiness, and turned aside into a lonely barn to wrestle with God; and while kneeling there on the threshing floor he gained a little light, but not enough to burst his bonds and set him free. Shortly after, however, in a prayer meeting, his eyes were opened to see all clearly. "I felt," he says, "that I was nothing, and Christ was all in all. Him I now cheerfully received in all his offices; my Prophet to teach me, my Priest to atone for me, my King to reign over me. O what boundless, boundless happiness, there is in Christ, and all for such a poor sinner as I am! This change took place, March 13th, 1772."

In pencil mark at the bottom of the page, in the memoir from which this extract is taken, a reader has noted "A second conversion precise as to time." This narration, however, is not given simply as an illustration of second conversion, but rather to meet the special pleading "not for me," on the ground that it is a special endowment for eminent ones. I wish to show that it is an endowment to make eminent ones. Often and often in the providence of God, it has taken men from the respectable ranks of mediocrity, or the low walks of obscurity, and lifted them to eminence.

Here is a youth just out of an apprenticeship to a farmer — a farmer's boy of all work, able to spell out a few words indeed upon the printed page, but unable to write a word or form a letter with the pen. Not an eminent one certainly; and yet he said, "It is for me — I must have it; and by the grace of God I will." And by the grace of God he did.

And now mark what follows. The fire kindled in that poor boy's heart burned so glowing and so gloriously, that the angel of the Lord took from that altar the living coals to touch the lips and purge the sins of thousands. Carvosso married and became a pilcher fisherman in the obscure fishing village of Mouse-hole on the coast of England — a fisher of men, too, and few more successful than he. Four months of the year he plied his seine for pilchers, but he caught pilcher catchers the whole year round. Their first chapel was a small room in a fisher's hut; the next an offensive fish-drying cellar; the next a large upper room, made ready, but so frail as to crumble and tumble and crash, a heap of ruins, under the weight of the first assembly. Numbers grew, and zeal with numbers and ability with zeal, and they built a fine chapel. The whole place was transformed.

Tired of fishing, he became a farmer. The parish where his farm lay was unbroken fallow ground; weeds rank, stones ungathered, fields unhedged, a heath in the desert. Soon, however, under the diligent hand of Carvosso, it began to blossom as the rose. The few scattered sheep grew into three flourishing classes. His hands were full. From abroad they sent for him, and at one place, Cambuslang, where he went from house to house through the day, and held class-meetings at night, seven hundred or more were hopefully converted to God.

For sixty years this farmer boy, made eminent by grace, wrought on. And yet, strange to say, until he was sixty-five years old, the forming of the letter P in his class-book, to mark the presence of the members of his classes, was his utmost effort in the art of writing. His wife used to rally him about penmanship saying, "All you can do is to make P's."

A simple circumstance induced him after he was sixty-five, to make extraordinary effort and learn to write. He mastered the art, and used it too. His letters and his autobiography are quite voluminous and very respectable in style; and, what is more than all, have been first and last the means, perhaps, of more good than his personal labors during all the sixty years of his distinguished usefulness. Comment is needless. Let Carvosso persuade you that faith and grace can raise even the obscure to eminence, while unbelief paralyzes even those distinguished for native abilities and superior opportunities and positions, and leaves them to float along in mediocrity or sink into obscurity.

This upon the assumption of your plea that this is a limited matter. But in fact, this assumption is entirely groundless. Nay, more. It limits God, and God's holy word, and God's boundless grace. Not for me? Why not? Is not Christ able? Is he unwilling? Are the promises limited? Are the commands binding only upon a few? Can any enter heaven without holiness? Is there any other way of becoming holy? Is your name mentioned as an exception in the promises and invitations of the Word? Do you find any such phenomena as a proclamation like this, "Look unto me, ye few, and be ye saved, for I am God?" Or like this, "Whosoever will, let him drink of the waters of life freely — except yourself?" or like this, "For the promise is, not unto you and your children, and to all that are afar off, even as many as the Lord our God shall call," but only to a few eminent ones, or a few of peculiar temperament, or a few in favorable circumstances?

Favorable circumstances! Not for me! My circumstances, my associations, my calling, my position so unfavorable! Ah, if only I was a minister with nothing to do but to do good, and study how to do it!

Now let another of the Lord's eminent ones witness for him.

*HENRY HAVELOCK.**

(* A friend objects to Havelock as an example, because he was a military man — a man of blood. And asks, "Can any man be a whole-hearted Christian, and yet a military man? Under the gospel economy of the Kingdom of God can any one deliberately select the profession of arms, or of his own choice remain in it, after his conversion, taking part in the bloody scenes of war as Havelock did, and yet live in the smiles of Divine approbation and love from day to day?")

The gallant soldier and heroic Christian Havelock, was converted on board the "General Kyd," outward bound for India. He was young, and only a lieutenant, with an untried sword both as a soldier and as a Christian, but destined to great deeds in both fields. His enlistment was as hearty under the banner of the Lion of the tribe of Judah, as under the lion of Britain, and his commission from the King of Heaven had the broad seal of authenticity in the assurance of sins forgiven, as undoubted and unequivocal as his commission from the King of his country. He landed at Calcutta a soldier of the cross. But there God had in store for him yet better things. It was not in Havelock's nature to hide his colors. His uniform did not more fully declare his profession a military man, than did his uniform Christian conduct, his position in the Church militant. Once fairly settled at Fort William, he sought out those in Calcutta, distinguished in the service of his own new found Captain and King, and his intercourse with them was greatly blessed. His conversion was on board the "General Kyd." It was then on the high seas that he was met by Him of whom the Psalmist said, "Help is laid upon one mighty to save, whose hand is in the tea." But now in the British Indian Capital, and in the Fortress the same glorious Saviour met him again, and opened his eyes more fully than ever and revealed himself to him anew. His biographer says of this second conversion, that, "The scriptures opened to him in yet greater fulness, and his consecration to his Master's service assumed yet greater intelligence and force."

Now Havelock would have been a distinguished soldier, and a decided Christian without doubt, even if he had not been met and blessed the second time as he was. But to understand the philosophy of his unswerving dauntlessness in religion, and the deep solicitude he felt for the conversion of his soldiers, and of the heathen, to find the source of the steady brilliance of his light, we must look to the two scenes, the first on the "General Kyd," but not less to the second in "Fort William," and see how there the living union was formed, first and then more fully opened, afterward by faith between him and his Saviour, that living union which like the tubes from the living olive trees in the vision of the prophet, poured the golden oil in constant current into the golden lamps, keeping their light ever fresh, never dim. His after life as a man, a soldier, and a Christian, was but the unfolding of the elements then fully set at work, to make him what he was, under the constant presence, and culture, and providence of his Captain and King.

Now suppose Havelock had said in the first instance, as doubtless he may have been tempted to say, and as some of his fellow-officers in the service, and fellow-voyagers in the General Kyd did probably say, "Not for me?" Or in the second instance — where now would have been the record which has thrilled all Christendom with wonder and delight, the record which is on high? Where? And yet he, a youth, and a subordinate officer, amongst scoffing fellow-officers, and amongst a soldiery not over devout or pure, going into a heathen land, and his trade war, and his profession ambition. Surely he might have exclaimed with a sigh of despair, "My circumstances! Oh, my circumstances! Not for me! not for me! " Yet it was for him, and it is for you too, if through unbelief you do not reject it. Again let me entreat you, weigh it well! Again let me ask you, can you reject it and be innocent.

But my temperament! With my perplexities and trials. Ah! my temperament would never allow me to live in it, if I should gain it." Of all the pleas put in by those already convinced of the reality and blessedness of full salvation, this is the most frequent; and the most plausible too to those who so plead, and yet of all it is the most foolish and groundless.

The plea in all reason and common sense ought to be reversed. It should be. Ah! my temperament and my temptations! I can never live unless I do have the fulness of faith, and the fulness of salvation. I must have it. Whatever others may do who have less to contend with, I must have it, and by the grace of God I will.

To make our very necessities a plea for rejecting instead of receiving it, is against all reason. Just as well might the poor cripple, who can only walk a few steps at a time without falling down, make that a plea for refusing the strong arm of a willing brother who offers to hold him up, and help him on to the end. And just as well might a poor sufferer gasping for breath in a close room, dying for want of air, refuse to have the free air let in, on the plea that he could not breathe with what he had already.

If all was right, temperament and temper, disposition and aim, position and circumstances, no Saviour would be needed. As it is, the more irritable our temperament, and irascible our temper, the more distracting our cares, and the more subtle and powerful our adversaries, and the worse our associations, the more we need a Saviour, and the more we need all the fulness of faith, and salvation.

Says He who walketh in glory amidst the golden candlesticks, "I counsel thee to buy of me gold tried in the fire, that thou mayest be rich; and white raiment, that thou mayest be clothed, that the shame of thy nakedness do not appear; and anoint thine eyes with eye salve, that thou mayest see. Behold I stand at the door and knock; if any man hear my voice, and open the door, I will come in to him, and will sup with him, and he with me. To him that overcometh I will give to sit with me upon my throne, even as I also overcame, and am set down with my Father on His throne."

"Rise! touched with love divine,
Turn out his enemy, and thine,
That soul destroying monster, sin,
And let the heavenly stranger in!"

This is a grave question in ethics, and involves also the still broader one of the allowability of war under any circumstances. Of course in a footnote questions so broad cannot be discussed at large. To answer the objection in a manner the briefest is all that can be thought of.

Is the objection good?

If it is good against Havelock, it is good also against Captain Vicars, Colonel Gardiner and General Burns — all men of valor, both in the cause of their country, and in the cause of their God.

Nay, more; if good against these, it is equally good against men highly commended in the New Testament for their devotion and faith.

The first Gentile to whom the gospel was preached, as a Gentile, was a Roman military officer, Cornelius, a centurion of the Italian Band, stationed at Cesarea, which was then the local seat of government and centre of military affairs for Judea. And the pen of inspiration commends him as devout, liberal, and prayerful, even before the Apostle Peter was sent to preach Christ to him at his house, and informs us that the Holy Spirit fell upon him and his household while Peter was speaking, just as at Pentecost He had come upon the apostles. And yet not one word is said to him, or of him, as if his profession of arms was against the ethics of the gospel.

And the man of all others most highly commended by our Saviour himself for his faith, was also a Roman military officer. He came to Jesus in the streets of Capernaum, and said to him "I am not worthy that thou shouldst come under my roof. Speak the word and my servant shall be healed. For I also am a man under authority, and I say to one, come, and he cometh, and to another, do this, and he doeth it."

Jesus listened to him. His appeal based its mustration upon his own military power and authority over his soldiers, but our Saviour did not condemn him for being a centurion. He listened with wonder and admiration, and turned him about to his followers saying, I have not found so great faith, no, not in Israel.

The presumptive testimony of these facts is altogether against the validity of the objection.

But there is a single thought which is sufficient both to show the baselessness of the objection and the consistency of these facts with the ethics of the gospel, and perhaps also to furnish the principle for the settlement of the general question, whether under the gospel economy there can be a justifiable war?

What are the army and the navy?

Are they not simply a national police?

Are they not to the nation at large — in principle — just what the civic police is to the city, and the sheriffalty and constabulary are to the country? The arm of the government for the protection of the honest and the peaceful, and for the arrest and punishment of the vile and the violent?

Is it right, or is it wrong, to have a police force on the high seas for the suppression of piracy and the traffic in slaves? To catch the sharks of commerce, and protect the weak and the exposed?

One thing of two must be. Every merchantman must be armed for self-defence, or the government must defend its merchantmen by a navy.

Is it right for the nation within its own borders to put down conspiracy, enforce its laws, preserve order, and protect innocent citizens?

Is it right to present a bulwark of honest hearts, strong hands and deadly weapons against the invader who comes to rob and destroy, to kill and lay waste?

Then it is right to have soldiers and sailors. And then it is right for some to be soldiers and sailors, and whole hearted ones too, if soldiers and sailors at all.

There is nothing in that to hinder being whole hearted Christians at the same time.

Is there anything wrong in being a justice, or alderman, or mayor, or judge, or governor, or president? No more is there in being a captain, or general or commodore.

Is there anything in the office of our civic police, if discharged honestly, boldly, prayerfully, to grieve the Spirit of God, or cause the frown of the Most High? No more is there in being a soldier or a sailor.

The question concerning any particular war, of course must turn upon the particular circumstances of the case. Each case must be judged of by itself, just as each civil suit, and each criminal prosecution must be separately judged.

Without question there is always wrong on one side if not on both. It could not be otherwise.

But the question concerning the constitutionality of the military under the economy of the gospel turns upon the necessity there is for a national police to hold the lawless, whether amongst nations, or amongst the separate communities of each nation in check, and for punishing the desperadoes who seek honor or gain at the expense of the honest and peaceful.

Taking this broad view of the subject, we at once see how Havelock, and Vicars, and Gardiner, and Burns could bask every day in the sunshine of God's favor, while at the same time they were honestly and earnestly doing their duty as soldiers, whether in camp, or on the march, or in the heat of the battle.

And we see, too, how the centurions could be commended, as they were, for their extraordinary devotion and faith, while yet they wore the uniform, and bore the commission of Roman military officers.

And we see, also, how John the Baptist could consistently answer the soldiers who came to him as Ike did. Soldiers came to him there on the banks of the Jordan, asking, "And what shall we do?" As if their case was different from that of citizens. Must we abandon the service of Caesar to enter the service of God? was perhaps the substance of their question. So at least the answer of John intimates. John told them to do violence to no man — accuse none falsely — and be content with their wages. That is, if you will serve God, the service of Caesar does not stand in your way if you will only not be seditious on account of your wages, nor rob any one, or accuse any falsely to get money, but be true God-fearing soldiers of Caesar at the same time that you are true soldiers of God.

Now, however, turning the tables, if this view is correct and the military profession is lawful and right, judged by the gospel itself, then the example of Havelock remains in full force. He could be, as indeed he was, a gallant hero in the defence of his national flag, and in the rescue of his imperilled fellow-countrymen and fellow-Christians, and also, and more nobly a hero, under the standard of the cross, and in the rescue of immortal souls from a fate more terrible than that of torture or massacre by Hindoo or Mussulman.

And his example is the more brilliant and noble from the fact that he rose above all the temptations of both peace and war, in an army and in a country, where faith and grace are tried to the utmost.

Havelock's is indeed an illustrious example, both from the lustre of his name and the lustre of his course, and from the dark sky out of which his star shone so steadily in its undimmed ever-increasing brilliance.

Part Two - How Attained

Chapter One - For Me: What Then Must I Do?

"THEN PETER SAID UNTO THEM, REPENT AND BE BAPTIZED EVERY ONE OF YOU IN THE NAME OF THE LORD JESUS CHRIST, FOR THE REMISSION OF SINS, AND YE SHALL RECEIVE THE GIFT OF THE HOLY GHOST." Acts ii: 38.

The Apostle Peter's answer to the question ["what must we do?"] of those pricked to the heart by his pungent words on the day of Pentecost, was substantially the same as the Apostle Paul's answer to the trembling, prostrate Philippian jailer, "Believe in the Lord Jesus Christ and thou shalt be saved."

John the Baptist taught repentance toward God and faith in the Messiah at hand, and his disciples, in pursuance of his teachings, were converted to God, receiving a change of heart by the regenerating power of the Holy Spirit. But at the same time, John taught his disciples that the Lord Jesus Christ — the one standing amongst them — the latchet of whose shoes the great prophet was not worthy to unloose — would baptize them with the Holy Ghost and with fire.

And when the Holy Ghost came upon the disciples of Jesus on the day of Pentecost, in the power of this new baptism, the Apostle Peter assured the wondering multitudes that it was Jesus, who being risen from the dead had shed forth this which they saw and heard. It was the ascension gift bestowed upon his disciples by the enthroned and glorified Messiah.

The Scriptures everywhere teach us the same thing. They always answer the question, "What must we do?" by the assurance, "Believe in the Lord Jesus Christ and thou shalt be saved." Whether the question relates to justification or sanctification the answer is the same. The way of freedom from sin is the very same, as the way of freedom from condemnation. Faith in the purifying presence of Jesus brings the witness of the Spirit with our spirits that Jesus is our sanctification, that the power and dominion of sin is broken, that we are free, just as faith in the atoning merit of the blood and obedience of Christ for us, brings the witness of the Spirit that we are now no longer under condemnation for sin, but freely and fully justified in Jesus.

In the next chapter the facts that Jesus is the all-sufficient Saviour, and that faith is the all-inclusive condition of salvation will be shown more at large. In this it may be well to guard against a misapprehension, almost sure to arise.

There may seem to be in what has already been said, and still more in what remains to be said, an engrossing of all the offices, attributes and relations of the Godhead — as we are interested in them — in the Son of God alone. God forbid that there should be even in appearance any robbery of the glory due to the Father and the Spirit. A few thoughts may serve now, to set this matter right before in appearance it shall have gone too far wrong.

The attentive reader of the Acts of the Apostles can hardly fail to see that if the title of that sacred book was changed to the Works of the Holy Spirit, instead of the Acts of the Apostles, it would be quite as appropriate as it now is. It opens with a history of the advent of the Spirit, on the day of Pentecost, and proceeds with an account of the fruits of this baptism in the boldness, energy, wisdom, and power of the Apostles, and in the activity, union, happiness, and fellowship of the disciples, and in the triumphs of the gospel. Everywhere it attributes to the Holy Spirit the government and guidance of the apostles. Separating them for their missions, hindering them when they essayed to go wrong, pointing out to them the right way, attending them with power in healing diseases, executing judgment, as in the case of Ananias and Sapphira, and giving efficacy to their words by falling upon those to whom they spoke while they were yet speaking, and, in general, carrying forward the whole work of God in the apostolic church. The Acts of the Apostles is really a history of the works of the Holy Ghost, just as the four gospels are the history of the life and teachings of the Lord Jesus Christ. At the same time the attentive reader must also see that the instructions dictated by the Holy Spirit himself; are always and only to believe on the Lord Jesus Christ, for salvation. So that while salvation is the work of the Holy Spirit, the Lord Jesus Christ, and not the Holy Spirit, is the object of faith for salvation. And why? Why, simply because the Holy Spirit is the gift of Jesus through faith in his name.

This is the historical teaching of the case. And this is in full harmony with the personal assurances of Jesus concerning it.

"On the last and great day of the feast, (of tabernacles) when Jesus stood (in the temple) and cried, saying, If any man thirst let him come unto me and drink. Whosoever believeth in me, as the Scriptures have said, out of his belly shall flow rivers of living water," it is added in explanation, "this spake he of the Spirit, which they that believe on him should receive, for the Holy Ghost was not yet given because that Jesus was not yet glorified." (St. John vii: 37-39).

And afterwards, just before his crucifixion, while promising the Holy Ghost as another comforter to his disciples to he given to them in his stead, our Saviour told them, that when he, the Spirit of truth is come, he will guide you into all truth: for he shall not speak of himself: but whatsoever he shall hear that shall he speak: and he will show you things to come. He shall glorify me: for he shall receive of mine, and shall show it unto you. All things that the Father hath are mine: therefore said I, that he shall take of mine, and shall show it unto you. (St. John XVI:13-15).

An intelligent minister of Jesus, whose experience is ripe, precious and full in the sweet influences of the Holy Spirit, in answer to the question, "How do you think of the Holy Spirit?" said "As Jesus Omnipresent." And his answer is in perfect accordance with the sacred word which calls the Holy Spirit the spirit of Jesus.

The modern Italian reformer, Gavazzi, a man of genius, amongst other stirring and significant things, delivered a discourse in London, entitled "Christ the justifier, Christ the sanctifier, Christ the glorifier." At first view this seems to be attributing to Christ the work of the Spirit; and so it is in the strict construction of the words in the form Gavazzi has given them. Literally and strictly the Holy Spirit and not Christ is the justifier, and sanctifier, and glorifier, for he it is who is the actual worker, the power that worketh in us, preparing the heart, producing the faith, and effecting the salvation in every step. But in the sense doubtless intended, Jesus is both justifier, sanctifier and glorifier; that is, he is the object of faith alike for each and all. And as the giver of the Holy Spirit he is the worker also of all.

In a sense perfectly true the artist who takes on likenesses in any form of the modern art of printing by light, is the daguerreotypist, or photographist, or whatever; but in a sense equally true it is the sun itself that does the work. The artist prepares the plate, arranges the instrument and the attitude, lets in the light and shuts it off again at the right moment, but it is the sun itself who by his rays takes every line and feature of the person, and dashes them all upon the plates. So while it is the work of the Spirit to prepare the heart, open it to the light and give the faith of Christ, it is Christ himself whose image is formed in the heart, the hope of glory. And who at the same time is himself the Sun of Righteousness unveiled by the Spirit, whose rays paint the image on the prepared tablet. According to the apostle's saying, that we all beholding Him as in a glass, are changed from glory to glory into his image even as by the Spirit of the Lord. (2 Corinthians iii. 18).

Strictly and literally, Jesus is our justification and sanctification and glorification; and the Holy Spirit is our justifier, sanctifier and glorifier. When therefore we trust wholly in Jesus for all, we do not rob the Holy Spirit of the honor justly his due, but we honor him by complying with his teachings and showing his work; for as the Scriptures have said, No man can say that Jesus is the Christ, (understanding what he says,) but by the Holy Ghost. So, likewise, by trusting wholly in Jesus, we honor also the Father. And this for two reasons, not to speak of others at present. First, Jesus is the express image of the Father — the Father's representative to us, the fulness of the Father made manifest to us in the flesh, and so honoring Jesus we honor the Father.

And then, again, the Father is the author and planner of salvation through faith in his Son; and when we trust in his Son we honor the Father, because we accept of his plan of salvation for us, justify his wisdom, and act, in accordance with his will in the matter. A glance at the official and essential relations of the persons of the Holy Trinity to each other and to us, may throw additional light upon our pathway. Upon this subject flippancy would border upon blasphemy. It is holy ground. He who ventures upon it may well tread with unshod foot, and uncovered head bowed low.

Speculation here, too, is entirely out of place, unsafe, not worth the ink used in the writing. The lamp of human reason is a light too dim to guide us through the profound mysteries of the mode of the divine existence and the methods of the divine manifestation and working. God alone knows what God is. And God only can communicate to man what man can be made to know of God, especially of the personalities of the Godhead, and of their relations to each other and to us.

Revelation must be our guide. Beyond what God has revealed, we know nothing. The sacred Word is all the light we have in this matter. In a sense scriptural, and true Christ is "all the fulness of the Godhead bodily." "The express image of the invisible God." "The fulness of Him who filleth all in all." The fulness of the Father and of the Spirit. In a sense equally scriptural and true, the Father is all the fulness of the Godhead; and so also is the Spirit.

The Father is the fulness of the Godhead in invisibility, without form, whom no creature hath seen or can see.

The Son is the fulness of the Godhead embodied, that his creatures may see him, and know him, and trust him.

The Spirit is the fulness of the Godhead in all the active workings, whether of creation, providence, revelation, or salvation, by which God manifests himself to and through the universe.

The counsels of eternity are therefore all hidden in the Father, all manifested by the Son, and all wrought by the Spirit. Let us glance first at the official relations of the persons of the Godhead. To gain something like distinct ideas of these divine relations we need to be lifted up in thought, as the eyes of the patriarch Jacob were at Bethel, by a ladder with its foot on the earth but its top in heaven. Such a ladder the Bible sets up before us in the names and similies of the persons and work, especially of the Son and the Spirit. The Son is called the Word, the Logos. Now a word before it has taken on articulate form is thought. The word is the express image of the thought, the fulness of the thought made manifest. So the Son is the fulness of the Godhead made manifest. The thought is the fulness of the word not yet made manifest. So the Father is the fulness of the Godhead invisible. Again the Spirit is like the thought expressed and gone forth to do its work of enlightening, convincing, changing. When a thought has been formed into words, risen to the tongue, fallen from the lips upon other ears, into other hearts, it works there its own full work. So the Holy Spirit is the fulness of the Godhead at work fulfilling the designs of God.

THE FATHER IS LIKE THE THOUGHT UNEXPRESSED.
THE SON IS LIKE THE THOUGHT EXPRESSED IN WORDS.
THE SPIRIT IS LIKE THE WORD WORKING IN OTHER MINDS.

Another of the names of Jesus will give the same analogies in a light not less striking — The Sun of Righteousness.

All the light of the sun in the heavens was once hidden in the invisibility of primal darkness; and after this, the light now blazing in the orb of day was, when first the command when forth, Let light be! and light was, at most only the diffused haze of the gray dawn of the morn of creation out of the darkness of chaotic night, without form, or body, or centre, or radiance, or glory. But when separated from the darkness and centered in the sun, then in its glorious glitter it became so resplendent that none but the eagle eye could bear to look it in the face.

But then again its rays falling aslant through earth's atmosphere and vapors, gladdens all the world with the same light, dispelling the winter, and the cold, and the darkness; starting Spring forth in floral beauty, and Summer in vernal luxuriance, and Autumn laden with golden treasures for the garner.

THE FATHER IS AS THE LIGHT INVISIBLE.
THE SON IS AS THE LIGHT EMBODIED.
THE SPIRIT IS AS THE LIGHT SHED DOWN.

One of the similies for the blessed influences of the SPIRIT while giving the selfsame official relations of the persons of the Godhead, to each other and to us, may illustrate them still further — The Dew — The dew of Hermon — the dew on the mown meadow. Before the dew gathers at all in drops, it hangs over all the landscape in invisible vapor, omnipresent but unseen. By and by as the night wanes into morning, and as the temperature sinks and touches the dew point the invisible becomes the visible, the embodied; and, as the sun rises, it stands in diamond drops trembling and glittering in the sun's young beams in pearly beauty upon leaf and flower, over all the face of nature.

But now again, a breeze springs up, the breath of heaven is wafted gently along, shaking leaf and flower, and in a moment the pearly drops are invisible again. But where now? Fallen at the root of herb and flower to impart new life, freshness, vigor to all it touches.

THE FATHER IS LIKE THE DEW IN INVISIBLE VAPOR.
THE SON IS LIKE THE DEW GATHERED IN BEAUTEOUS FORM.
THE SPIRIT IS LIKE THE DEW FALLEN TO THE SEAT OF LIFE.

Yet one more of these Bible likenings — by no means exhausting them — will not be unwelcome or useless — the Rain.

Rain, like the dew, floats in invisibility, and omnipresence at the first, over all, around all. Seen by none. While it remains in its invisibility, the earth parches, clods cleave together, the ground cracks open, the sun pours down his burning heat, the winds lift up the dust in circling whirls, and rolling clouds, and famine gaunt and greedy stalks through the land, followed by pestilence and death. By and by, the eager watcher sees the little hand-like cloud rising far out over the sea. It gathers, gathers, gathers; comes and spreads as it comes, in majesty over the whole heavens: — But all is parched and dry and dead yet, upon earth.

But now comes a drop, and drop after drop, quicker, faster — the shower, the rain — sweeping on, and giving to earth all the treasures .of the clouds — clods open, furrows soften, springs, rivulets, rivers, swell and fill, and all the land is gladdened again with restored abundance.

THE FATHER IS LIKE TO THE INVISIBLE VAPOR.
THE SON IS AS THE LADEN CLOUD AND PALLING RAIN.
THE SPIRIT IS THE RAIN — FALLEN AND WORKING IN REFRESHING POWER.

These likenings are all imperfect. They rather hide than illustrate the tri-personality of the one God, for they are not persons but things, poor and earthly at best, to represent the living personalities of the living God. So much they may do, however, as to illustrate the official relations of each to the others and of each and all to us. And more. They may also illustrate the truth that all the fulness of Him who filleth all in all, dwells in each person of the Triune God.

THE FATHER IS ALL THE FULNESS OF THE GODHEAD INVISIBLE.
THE SON IS ALL THE FULNESS OF THE GODHEAD MANIFESTED.
THE SPIRIT IS ALL THE FULNESS OF THE GODHEAD MAKING MANIFEST.

The persons are not mere offices, or modes of revelation, but living persons of the living God. *(Olshausen in his commentary, vol. ii. p. 310, Am. edition, on John 1:3, makes a profound suggestion of the relation between the Father and the Son, well worthy of being expanded, and weighed with all candor and care.)*

Now as to the essential relations of the three, the Scriptures speak of each precisely as if each were living person, and not a mere official relation of the one person in three different connections, or adaptations. And we are also fully justified in the belief that in the personalities of the living God, in whom is all the fulness of all things, society exists. The beau-ideal of society as it is but imperfectly wrought out in the social relations of angels and men. Society in its first and highest form, first and best of all in the Godhead. And society amongst the creatures of God in its best estate, but a feeble and yet a noble image of its blessedness and glory as it is in the perfect social relations of the perfect three in one.

To go fully into the Scripture proofs, justifying these statements, would break the thread of our general course. To say this much seemed necessary lest the reader should be stumbled by the thought that the glory due to the Father and the Spirit was all given to the Son. Enough has been said to show the way clear for full trust in Jesus for full salvation. There is no fear of honoring the Father or the Spirit too little by honoring the Son too much. The deeper and fuller and stronger our trust in Jesus, the sweeter and richer the indwelling presence of the Spirit will be. And the more we have of the indwelling presence and in-working power of the Spirit, the higher our love and veneration will rise for the Father. Having the Son we have the Father also. And trusting the Son we receive the Spirit who reveals to us the Father and the Son. Full trust in Jesus therefore, brings the full revenue of honor due to the Father and the Son and the Spirit, while, from the Triune God's grace, mercy and peace are multiplied to us, and so the angelic song is fulfilled —- "Glory to God in the highest, and on earth peace and good will to men."

To return for a moment to the Apostle, and to the Pentecostal scene: Once when Peter was in self-confident mood the Master told him, that Satan had desired to have him that he might sift him as wheat, but that he had prayed for him that his faith should not fail: and he added the prophetic charge: "When thou art converted — that is converted again, for already long before Peter had been converted — strengthen thy brethren."

Satan did have the Apostle, and did sift him, too, but the prayer of Jesus was answered nevertheless. Peter was sifted but saved, as many others have been. The chaff of self-confidence was all threshed off and winnowed away, leaving the wheat in its naked integrity.

By and by, on the day of Pentecost, the time came for the apostle's second conversion. The Holy Spirit — the promise of the Father was received by the Son and shed down upon him and his fellow disciples. Fire crowns sat upon their heads, and with other tongues they spake of the wonderful works of God. These tongues of fire and tongues of eloquence were, however, only the outside symbols and the outspoken manifestations of the glorious work wrought in their hearts. They knew something of Jesus before — but now for the first they began to comprehend the length and breadth and depth and height — and to know the love of Christ which passeth knowledge, and to be filled with all the fulness of God. And now for the first the wisdom of God in the plan of redemption began to unfold to their view. Great as were the external signs of that work the internal work itself was far greater. And it was the beginning of a life-long process, in the course of which, more and more, from day to day, the things of God were unfolded to them, and more and more they were transformed into the image of Jesus.

This for themselves. Then also began the promised power, with them of witnessing effectively for Jesus. That very day, what a work was wrought by means of their testimony.

The fame of these things was noised abroad, from street to street through the city, and multitudes thronged to the temple to see and hear these strange things for themselves. Many believed and received like baptism from on high. Others mocked, saying, "These men are filled with new wine." This charge of drunkenness — a blasphemy against God who wrought it, and a slander upon the disciples in whom the glorious excitement was wrought — brought Peter quickly to his feet. Now he was ready to obey the Master's sacred command. He rose amidst his brethren — in the full strength, and glow, and boldness of his new conversion — to strengthen and defend them, and give glory to God.

The adversaries were silenced by his arguments, and cut to the heart by the charges boldly brought against them as the betrayers and murderers of the Lord of glory — the Lord Jesus, who had shed down the Holy Spirit whose works they saw and heard.

Some gnashed on him in their rage, but others were stricken down into contrition, and when in broken-hearted penitence, they earnestly inquired what they should do, Peter directed them at once to Jesus as the sole object of trust, telling them to "Repent and be baptized in the name of the Lord Jesus Christ," and assuring them that they should "receive the Holy Ghost." Thousands believed, and obeyed, and realized the promise in their own happy experience.

A great work was wrought on that day — a work to be had in everlasting remembrances. Many were then for the first time convinced of their sins and converted to God. Many more who had already been converted under the preaching of John the Baptist, and of Jesus himself, and of the twelve, and the seventy, were converted anew, and filled with faith and the Holy Ghost. And one thing may be safely affirmed of both alike, those converted again, and those now converted for the first, that in every case, trust in Jesus was the sole condition of the work wrought in them.

The apostle Peter did not say to the one, Believe in the Lord Jesus and ye shall be converted, and to the other, Watch, pray, struggle, read, fast, work, and you shall be sanctified. But to one and all he said, Repent and be baptized, every one of you, in the name of the Lord Jesus Christ, and ye shall receive the Holy Ghost. And yet another thing may be as safely affirmed of them all alike; that every one who did really believe and obey did actually receive the Holy Spirit, whether in the power of first or second conversion. Wherefore as the sum of all, let it be settled as truth never to be doubted, that for salvation in any stage or degree

Jesus alone is The Way,
And Faith alone is the Means.

Connected with this line of thought there is one thing more to be noted, which must conclude this chapter. There is often a fearfulness in addressing prayer to Christ and to the Holy Spirit. Frequently the devout and earnest worshipper appeals to Christ and then checks himself as if it were wrong, and turns in his appeal to the

Father in the name of the Son, as if afraid that the appeal to the Son might be offensive to the Father.

This fear is groundless. When, in the days of his flesh, Jesus was appealed to, whether for light and instruction, or for healing power, or whatever, none were ever checked by him for it. Peter sinking in the water cried out, "Lord save or I perish!" and Jesus rebuked him for his unbelief, but not for calling upon him instead of the Father. The Syrophenician woman appealed to him in behalf of her daughters and although the Lord tried her faith exceedingly, first by silence, then by saying "It is not meet to give the children's bread to dogs;" yet when she persevered, and said, "Truth Lord," you are right, I am not worthy, "Yet even the dogs eat of the crumbs that fall from the master's table," Jesus commended her, saying, "O woman! great is thy faith! Be it unto thee even as thou wilt;" and her daughter was healed from that hour.

And when, after the Lord's resurrection and ascension to glory, he met the persecuting Saul of Tarsus on the Damascus road, and rebuked him, saying, "Saul! Saul! why persecutest thou me?" Saul, fallen upon his face, and stricken blind by the glory of the Lord, tremblingly inquired, "Who art thou, Lord?" The answer was, "I am Jesus whom thou persecutest." Then Saul, obedient to the heavenly vision, asked, "Lord what wilt thou have me to do?" And Jesus answered, saying, "Go into the city and there it shall be told thee what thou must do." Then after three days, Ananias came to him, saying, "Saul! Jesus who met thee in the way hath sent me to thee, that thou mayest receive thy sight;" upon which as it were scales fell from his eyes. Now in all this there was no going round about, no feeling of necessity for it, no rebuke from the Lord for not doing it. When the earnest soul appeals directly to Jesus it will not be rebuked or sent away empty. And the same may be said of appeals to the Father direct, or to the Spirit.

When, in the language of that precious hymn, Rock of Ages, we in the same breath praise and pray:

"Rock of Ages cleft for me
Let me hide myself in thee,"

We are in the spirit of the gospel and in the line of perfect propriety. And so when we at one and the same moment invoke the Spirit and make melody unto God with heart and voice, saying:

"Come Holy Spirit Heavenly Dove,
With all Thy quickening powers,
Kindle a flame of sacred love
In these cold hearts of ours."

We are in no more danger of offending the Father than when, in the words put upon our lips by the blessed Saviour himself, we pray,

"Our Father who art in heaven."

In each and every case of the three the appeal is direct to the person of the trinity addressed, and in all alike proper, amid in all alike availing, if the plea is the fervent effectual outgoing of the heart in its fulness.

On critical grounds, as inadmissible without manifest violence to the text, he discards the Sabellian idea of no distinction, save that of office, between the Father and the Son; and also the Arian idea, on the other extreme, of a distinction not only, but of an inequality both of honors and powers, the Son being intermediate between God and man, a sort of divine creature.

And then putting together the two definite doctrines well established by the Scriptures, the unity of God, and the perfect equality of the Father and the Son in honors, and in properties, together with the clear distinction between the two, shown by the fact that the Son was not only God, but was also with God in the beginning; he remarks that these afford an idea of the relation of the Son to the Father, viz., that the Son is the self-manifestation of the Father to himself, or the perfect conception of himself imaged forth to himself. "The perfect God forms a perfect conception of himself, his conception is essence, and his conception of himself is an essence like himself." These are his words.

A moment's consideration of the difference between God and man, as to the embodiment of their respective conceptions, will show the profound beauty of this suggestion of the learned commentator, whether his idea shall be received as true or not.

The conceptions of men are only imperfectly realized in their productions. A man's own conception of himself may be partially embodied in a statue chizzled from the marble. But however perfect he may make it as a work of art, it is all imperfection as a realization of his own conception of himself. It is only a cold, lifeless, colorless piece of marble at last, and not at all the living being, bodied in his own idea of what he himself is. He may make a better representation of himself on the canvas, if his is the skill of the painter, and the genius of the Master but the best he can do after all, with the genius of a Raphael, or a Reynolds, will be no more than a painted representation of the picture of his own real self, in his own living conception.

Better still he may do, if his is the pen of the ready writer and the genius of a Shakespeare to depict in action, by word and deed, his own true character; but even then, his is only a pen and ink man in a book at last, and not at all the living man in the living world, of his own true conception of himself. Even if represented by the skill of a Keene, or a Kemble, on the stage to the very life, it is only a mock of reality, and not reality at all.

But God's conception of himself, is himself perfectly bodied forth to himself, and with himself, a living, acting being, or his conception of himself realized in actual existence, and not in mere representation.

God's ideas embodied, are all realities, not representations. His idea of a rock for example, when embodied, is a rock, and not a mere picture, or description, or imitation of a rock, as any representation by man of his idea of a rock would be. God's idea of a world when embodied is a world, and not a papier mache globe, or an outspread map, or an elaborate description. God's idea of the great orrery above and around us, embodied as it is, is this mighty universe of real suns and systems, and not a mere celestial map, or a magic lantern representation.

God's conception of living beings, and living scenes, such as have come upon the stage, from that first scene of love and loveliness in Eden, and the fall, onward to the end when the recovery shall be celebrated in the Eden above, embodied is not a mere poetic, dramatic, and scenic embodiment, like Milton's and Shakespeare's conceptions, but the realities as conceived, coming on the stage of actual life, in the solemn march of truthful existence.

Just so God the Father's conception of himself, is himself realized in form, or imaged forth, not in mere representation by description, but in actual living existence, a divine person, as real an existence as he is himself. And this living being, the embodiment of the Father's own conception of himself is the Son. The Son of God, and he embodied in the man, incarnated and born of the virgin is also the son of man, as well as the Son of God.

And in the same way God the Father's own conception of himself, working in the actual process of creating, sustaining, and redeeming — of himself working all things according to the counsel of his own will is, himself, his other self so to speak, a real being, truly personal as either himself or his Son, with every attribute, natural and moral, all complete, entire, wanting nothing. And this being, the God working all things is the Holy Spirit; and he like the Son, is both coequal and coeternal with the Father.

This is the commentator's suggestion expanded. Weigh it at your leisure. If we accept it as truth, it will harmonize some things, in the Sacred Word apparently in conflict, and free others from obscurity. Nevertheless in this matter of the essential relations of the divine persons in the Holy Trinity, we do well to be not over confident, not at all dictatorial or alogmatic, but modest and moderate.

In this view, we can easily see how the Scripture order of the persons of the Trinity come to be as they are in the record, and always so. The Father, the Son, and the Holy Ghost, because from the Father proceed both the Son and the Holy Ghost. And we can see how the three are each equal to each and to all, for the Son is the Father in all his fulness imaged forth. And the Spirit is the Father working or making manifest the Deity as imaged forth in the Son, and all the planes of the Deity in the works of creation, having the Son for the centre of all.

And we can see at the same time, how the Son though equal with the Father, can yet be subordinate to him, working only the works given him to do, and doing always the will of the Father, and being in fact less than the Father — that is officially less — because his office work in the Divine economy is subordinate, although all power is given him on earth, and in heaven. And we can see how, while Jesus is the giver of the Holy Spirit to all who believe on his name, yet the Holy Spirit is promised as from the Father, for he is both from the Father, and yet he is the ascension gift of the Son.

And we can see how the Holy Spirit can be, and is equal with both the Father and the Son, while yet he is officially subordinate to both, sent by the one given by the other, and glorifying both, but not speaking of himself.

And we can see how the Son and the Spirit can be truly said both to proceed from God, and yet to have been with God, and to have been God from the beginning, that is from eternity. For from eternity, God's conception of himself both as embodied and imaged forth in the word, and as working out his own counsels in the created universe, was perfect, and these conceptions were perfectly realized, and were the Son and the Spirit.

And finally, to come back to our starting point, the paradox which gave birth to this suggestion, we see the consistency of the apostle's sayings, that in the beginning the Word was with God, and was God, and the same was in the beginning with God. For from the first the word was formed in the Infinite mind, and was the Infinite mind embodied in the form, and imaged forth to itself, at one and the same time himself God, and yet with God.

Chapter Two - Christ All-Sufficient and Faith All-Inclusive

THE ANALOGIES OF FIRST AND SECOND CONVERSION — DIFFERENCE — CHRIST ALL — A SON OF THE PROPHETS AT A SCHOOL OF THE PROPHETS — FAITH TWO-FOLD, GIVES ALL — A LADY OF DISTINCTION, TAKES ALL — A MERCHANT.

The analogies between conversion and second conversion, are complete in all things — save one.

There is a radical difference between the pardon of sins, and the purging of sins. Pardon is instantaneously entire, but cleansing from sin is a process of indefinite length. Even here, however, the analogy, though not complete, is not entirely wanting, for in the second as in the first, the apprehension of Christ as the way, is instantaneous, the difference being simply that in the first, the work of Christ is already done the instant the soul believes, while in the second, the work of Christ remains yet to be done in the future after the soul believes. In the one the atonement has been made, and the moment it is accepted, the pardon is complete; in the other, although the righteousness of Christ is perfect in which the soul is to be clothed yet the work of unfolding the heart to itself in its wants, and the unfolding of Christ to the heart from glory to glory, in his sympathizing love, and purifying presence and power, as the soul shall be prepared to go onward and upward from faith to faith, is a work of time and progress.

With this single exception, however, the analogies are complete. The period and process of conviction; the unwillingness at first to admit the light and obey the truth; the resolve afterward to seek and find the salvation; the vain attempts and fruitless struggles; the deceptions and temptations of the adversary; the final perception of Christ as the way, and the giving of all up to him, and taking him for all; the light, and comfort, and peace that follow, and the wonder that there should ever have been a single doubt of the reality that there is such an experience; and the wonder still greater, that the way of faith in Christ, so plain and so simple as it is should not have been seen at once first of all: in all these things the analogy is perfect, no shade of difference.

The experience in no case will be exactly the same in the second, as in the first. The experiences of no two persons are precisely alike in every feature, or in any one feature. No two have faces alike. All have faces, however, if they are human. No two have any one feature precisely the same, yet all have the same features. He who should have two mouths, or three eyes, or two noses, would be a monster, not a man. And he who should have no mouth, or nose, or eyes, at all, would be a deformed man at best. So in religious experience, all have the same general features, though no two are exactly alike. And this analogy of unity in diversity holds good between first and second conversion in any person's experience, the same as between the experiences of different persons.

We have here also, a correspondence with all the processes of nature. A seed germinates in the ground and shoots up its stem and bud to the light, where it unfolds itself to the sun, and the dews, and the air, and drinks in the power of a second germination; and then puts forth another bud and stem just like the first in every essential thing, while yet no two buds are ever exactly the same, and so grows by repeating itself. The same analogy might be traced through all the mineral kingdom, in all crystalline formations, and through all geological history.

This analogy as it chiefly concerns us for the great practical purpose in view, gives us, if we have passed through the first step, two things to guide us through the second, in the strong light of our own past experience. First, CHRIST AS ALL-SUFFICIENT, and second, FAITH AS ALL-INCLUSIVE.

The first grand effort of the convicted, burdened heart, is to find relief — not by taking Christ, at once as all-sufficient — not, perhaps, by going to Christ at all, until driven to him by repeated failures, at the work of changing itself. And when at last driven to him, then the first thing is — not to take Christ himself — but to seek is salvation rather than himself.

It is a very simple lesson to learn — as it seems when once it is learned — but one of the hardest we ever learn in our lives; that having Christ we have salvation also, while without receiving Christ himself we cannot have the salvation. Having the fountain we have its issuing -- streams. Cut off from the fountain, the streams will not flow to us. Christ offers himself to be the bridegroom of the soul. He offers to endow his bride with all the riches of his own inheritance in the heirship of his Father. Taking him as our bridegroom, and giving ourselves to him as the bride espouses her husband, with him we have all he has, as well as all he is, while without him we can have neither.

The mistake is that of seeking the salvation instead of seeking the Saviour. Just the same mistake that the affianced would make, if she should seek to have the possessions of him to whom she was engaged, made over to her from him, without their union in wedlock, instead of accepting his offer of himself, and having the hymenial bond completed, by which he and all he has would become hers.

Our salvation is IN Christ and with him, but not APART from him. When a bank note or a gold coin is put into my hands, my money is in that, not apart from it. When a deed is signed, sealed, recorded, and delivered to me, my title is in my deed and not apart from it. My bank note or gold coin will pay my debt and pay my journeying expenses. My deed will ensure me my farm. Even so in Christ I have my debt cancelled, my journeying support, and my heavenly inheritance all secure.

Perhaps this matter cannot be better illustrated than by a sketch of the struggles and victory of

ONE OF THE SONS OF THE PROPHETS AT ONE OF THE SCHOOLS OF THE PROPHETS.

J. was doubly one of the sons of the prophets. His father was a distinguished minister, and a professor in one of our so-called universities, while he himself was a student in one of our Theological Seminaries in this favored land. He was about to leave the halls of sacred science and go out to try his armor and his arms on the great western missionary battlefield. His conversion was clear and decided, years before while in college. His consecration to the ministry of Jesus was unwavering. His course as a young Christian and student had commended him to universal respect. The distinguished men who were training the sons of the prophets for their great work, esteemed J., even above most of the noble young m en around them. To all others his prospects were bright and fair, but J. had his own misgivings. When he thought of the great work of the ambassador for Christ, his heart chilled with fear lest he should come short. Then he turned himself to see what could be done. Resolutions — the first grand resort always — were formed, and alas, broken too, almost before they were cold. A covenant was written out, and signed, and sealed, and blotted with tears. But alas, again it proved worth not so much as the foolscap on which it was drawn up. Then it was nailed up in plain view of himself and his visitors in his own study, right over the desk where he dug out his Hebrew, and wrote out, his sermons. But the case was no better at last. Finally he vowed — a rash vow — to give his most splendid books, the treasure of his study, to the flames, if he should fail to keep covenant again with the Lord and his own soul. But he failed again. Now what? Now he did not know what. He was at his wit's end. He was a strong man of iron will. Unbending as the oak in his uprightness, and rooted deeply in all Biblical science — but his heart! Ah, his wayward heart was too much for him! He was associated with a fellow student in a Mission Sabbath School, and various other works of love for the cause of the Master. His fellow student, like Rieu with D'Aubigne, though far behind J. in many things, was far ahead of him in the knowledge of Jesus. In one of their conversations, his associate mentioned the fact of a second conversion, in the case of one mutually esteemed by them, and seeing a look of surprise in the face of J., said, "You know there is such an experience, do you not?" "No" answered J., "I do not. I never heard of such a thing." "Well then, be assured there is." Explanation followed, and they separated. Next time they met, the matter was called up again, and as they parted again, J. said, in tones of deepest emotion,"Come to my room as soon as you can. I shall die if I do not find relief from my agony of soul."

Next day, seated in J.'s room, a scene occurred between the two, never to be forgotten by either. J.'s anxiety seemed to have reached the highest point of endurance. The heartstrings were evidently ready to break. He wanted, he must have the fulness of the blessings of the gospel. He could live no longer without, so he said, and so he felt.

His friend pointed him to Jesus, saying, "Look to Jesus! Accept of Jesus! He offers himself to you to be yours. Take him at his word. Trust in him, and he will be all in all to you."

"Ah, yes, but that does not help me at all. I am not changed at all by that. I want to be changed, made all new. I am so vile! so fickle! so foolish! O, for transforming power!"

"No, but if you take Jesus to yourself as yours, and give yourself to him to be his, that is all you need. He will take you as you are, and keep you by his own mighty power through faith unto salvation."

"Ah! But, my heart! my heart! O, that is the same as ever! Tell me how my heart can be made anew!"

"Trust in Jesus. His covenant is, 'I will write my law in your heart. I will put my truth in your mind, and ye shall be my people, and I will be your God.' Trust in Jesus."

"Ah, yes, but that does not change me!"

"But is not Jesus able to do for you all he promises — all you ask or think? Think of his works of mercy, and wonders of love in the days of his flesh. He is with you now, as he was with his disciples then, only now in spirit, then in body; but yet, to do all you need, or can desire in the way of salvation. If you have him, you have all he can do for you, and will ever have. He will be with you, and be yours — your own — your Almighty Saviour — always everywhere. O, think what a treasure you have in Jesus!"

The Lord opened his eyes to see that Jesus was his, and that Jesus was all in all to him, more than file had ever dared to hope for. And hiding his face in his handkerchief, to prevent the convulsions of his features being seen, he sobbed out, "Oh! is that it? Is that it? Glorious! Glorious!"

Then after a moment, dropping on his knees, "Let us pray," he said. And slowly, yet as fast as he could control his utterance, he thanked God over, and over, and over, and over again for the unspeakable gift of such a Saviour to be the sinner's own, and all his own, and always his own, and all he ever could want in life and in death, to atone for his sins, and take away his sins, to justify him, and sanctify him, and glorify him. He could do nothing but praise, only just to exclaim, "O, that all might see him, and know him, and glorify him too!" This to him was a new and glorious era. He went forth to the battle, but not alone; and he lives to fight, but not alone. The invisible but Almighty Saviour is ever with him, and he knows it. Jesus is now all-sufficient, he wants no more, for in him, and with him "all things are his, whether life or death, or things present, or things to come," all are his, and he is Christ's, and Christ is God's.

FAITH ALL-INCLUSIVE.

This is the second matter of chief importance to be illustrated. True and saving faith is two-fold. It gives all and takes all. If it fails to give all up to Christ, no matter how bold and clamorous it may be in claiming the promises, it is dead and powerless. Its boldness, like Peter's before the crucifixion, will be put to shame when put to the test, and its owner will have occasion of bitter weeping in this world, and it may be of terrible gnashing of teeth in the world of despair. On the other hand if it of taking Christ for all, all its givings will be in vain, ending only in sore and terrible disappointment at last.

The word of God presents to us two grand assets. One of command and the other of promise. Faith trusts implicitly in both. Faith obeys the one accepts the other. In the Commandments, God himself as a requiring God — in the promises as a giving God. Faith relies upon Him, in his commandments and his promises — yielding explicit obedience to the one, and putting forth hand of assured confidence to take the other.

Now, that faith is not properly faith at all, which accepts the one and rejects or neglects the other.

God demands of us heart and life wholly given and consecrated to him, and true faith responds "Yes, Lord, Thou shalt have all. All I have and am are thine."

God gives us his Son to be our Saviour, and true faith takes him at once and for all in all, and is satisfied saying

"Thou O Christ art all I want,
More than all in Thee I find."

He who gives all and takes all has all. He who but does not take, or takes but does not give, has nothing but disappointment and sorrow.

Daniel obeyed the Lord and trusted in him. When the collision came between the command of the King and the command of God, Daniel's faith did not waver. He obeyed God rather than man. And when the test of the den and the lions came his faith was still unshaken; he trusted in Him whom he served.

Now for the sake of the illustration, suppose the faith of this noble servant of God had been reversed — suppose when the commands of the king and of God came into collision — he had done as, alas, too many do, obeyed man rather than God, and yet trusted to the clemency of God that he would not be angry with him, even though he did disobey — made the goodness of God a plea of presumption that all would be well at last, though the word of God was set at nought. Would God, think you, have left such a testimony on record as the exclamation of the angel: "O Daniel! Man greatly beloved of the Lord?" Or on the other hand, suppose when Daniel was cast into the lion's den, instead of trusting in his God, that he would deliver him — suppose then that in his impotence, bound hand and foot, he had made fight with the lions, and sought deliverance by his own struggles with those terrible beasts of prey, how long before he would have been torn limb from limb and devoured by the hungry monsters of the den? But no. When the commandment came up, Daniel made God his trust and obeyed, even at the risk of what seemed inevitable and terrible death. And when the danger came then again he made God his trust, and was delivered.

The two aspects and their results of Faith separated, may be illustrated by two separate sketches — First, a sketch of the struggles and failures, and final success of...

A LADY OF DISTINCTION

...will show the futility of trusting to the promises while neglecting the commandments, that is, the necessity for consecration to God in order to realize the saving power and presence of Jesus.

The lady in question is well known both in Europe and America, both by the brilliance of her genius, and the liberality of her gifts, but as she still living, her name is withheld.

For many years after her conversion, which was bright and clear and happy, she served the Lord in the too frequent sort of a life of ups and downs — knowing of nothing better for the Christian here below, at least for the Christian of her "temper and temperament," as she was wont to say. The superior consistency and fervor seen in some others, she thought was due mainly to superior natural qualities and educational training, rather than to any deeper and fuller experimental oneness with Christ.

A brother beloved however, at last convinced her that, for all the children of God, herself amongst the number of course, there is such an experimental union with Jesus as has for convenience been named second conversion.

Months wore away after this, however, before any earnest step was taken to make it her own. Notwithstanding her deep persuasion of its reality, for herself it seemed an impossible height to scale. Often and often it was called up in the heart's own ball of legislation, and as often with a sigh of despondency it was laid on the table again.

At last, meeting with one zealous in this matter, in whose mind the one aspect of faith — that of taking the promises, seemed in the main like Aaron's rod, to have swallowed up everything else, especially the other aspect — that of consecration, she was persuaded to cast herself upon Christ. And right heartily and wholly she did seem to take him to herself, and her hopes were sanguine that he would be to her and do for her all he had promised, and all that others received.

A little while, and her hopes all died. The Saviour seemed no nearer, no dearer, no more her helper than before.

Then came another similar trial, with similar results. And another, and another, and so on. More than a year passed in these fruitless struggles, and many a sad, sad disappointment marked and blotted the pages of that year's history. The hand of the Lord, always near at the right moment, at last placed upon her pillow — for she was ill at the time — Upham's "Interior Life." She read as she had strength to read, a few pages at a time. Coming to the chapter on " Consecration," she read it to the end, and said to herself, "This I have not done. I have tried to trust in Jesus, but I have never yet in all these attempts, made an entire surrender of myself to him, to do his will, but only to receive his salvation."

Turning back she re-read every line and every word with renewed care, and closer scrutiny. And as she read, the length and breadth of the requirements of God upon her, came out in appalling proportions. "Right! Right! Yes, all right," she said. "I ought to make this full consecrations of myself to God. But O, how hopeless! My whole pathway in the past, in memory, is strewn with the fragments of broken resolutions. And resolve I resolve again?"

The book recommended a written covenant, if convenient. After days and days of weary reflection, she concluded finally to make the covenant of consecration as advised. The first time she took to the easy chair as a rest from her long, long, prostration — even for an hour — she called for pen and ink, and wrote out a covenant, full even to the minutest details, signed it, and knelt and repeated it word from the heart, then rose exhausted and sought again her pillow.

Days passed by. Days of heavenly peace. Trials came, but her "peculiar temper and temperament" did not overcome her. She was calm as Silver Lake at sunrise and as bright and clear. She was slow to believe, after so many failures, that success had crowned this last act. By and by, however, the conviction that Jesus was with her, and was keeping her in perfect peace, and would do it, was forced upon her. And her joy in Jesus as a present Saviour — All-sufficient — was unbounded.

From the very first, she had been willing and more than willing that the Saviour should work in her to will and to do of his own good pleasure. And she was really convinced, fully persuaded that if ever the law of God should be written upon her heart in letters of light and love, it would be by the hand of God himself in answer to faith in Jesus. In this she was clear. She had no confidence in the flesh — none in her own will — none in any round of duties or course of action. She knew that God alone could fill her heart and soul with God. Why then, and how, did she fail? Simply because she did not yield herself a living sacrifice unto God. She gave herself up as a dead, a passive sacrifice merely. She consecrated herself to receive merely, and not to do. God requires of his intelligent voluntary creatures an intelligent active consecration to himself, heart and soul yielded to do his will, as well as receive his gifts of grace and mercy.

And in this, with all her genius and intelligence, and all her earnestness besides, she failed entirely until, through failure after failure, together with the timely suggestions of Professor Upham's Interior Life, she was led to review the past, and superadd a covenant of consecration to her covenant of trust for grace. Then, but not before, she came to the place to receive what the Lord had in store to bestow upon her.

Here then, in the case of this lady, we have a clear illustration of the necessity of that aspect and phase of faith, which obeys the command of God — which gives up heart and soul to do the will of God.

"Take my yoke," says our Saviour," and learn of me, for I am meek and lowly and you shall find rest to your souls. "But without taking the yoke, where is the learning and the rest of the soul? " "Whosoever will do the will of my Father shall know of the doctrine," he says again. But is not the converse of this saying equally true that, Whosoever will not do His will, shall not know the salvation?

The need of taking all, as well as giving all will be seen as clearly in another example, that of...

A MERCHANT

Early in life, at the very outset of a somewhat extended and varied business career, B. enlisted in the grand enterprise of laying up his treasures in heaven. At first, and for a while, he was quite content to make the Lord Jesus his chief banker, and counsellor, and was very joyous in his course as well as abundantly useful. From early childhood, however, the love of money, not for its own sake but for the glory of it, had been instilled into B.'s heart, and the habit of mercantile ambition had grown with his growth into the strength of an almost unconquerable desire. Kept under for a time after his conversion, this besetting sin by and by, like the shoots from Carvosso's stump in his garden, began to show itself. But unlike Carvosso, B: was not alarmed by it, and did not attempt even to pull up the noxious sprout. Satan reasoned him into its cultivation. "Get rich," said the tempter, "and O how much good yon can do with your money. Get rich and you will be a great man. Every body will respect you. Your influence will be mighty for good." "Yes," said B., "I will. I will never rest until I am the master of a fortune, and at the top of the topmost business circle."

A little circumstance helped this decision mightily. One of B.'s old school-mates who had been a sad laggard at school, and no better in business, when he heard of B.'s conversion, said, "Well, that will spoil him, he might have made a business man if he had let religion alone, but that will kill him. He'll never be much now."

This repeated to B., made him feel in his heart, "He shall see! My religion shall not spoil me! He will yet see, and all the world will see. I will be at the top yet."

His ambition was fired, and as the fire of ambition kindled into a flame in his heart, the fire of love sunk into ashy embers. He made money rapidly, and with money came pride and vanity. The valley of humility had little attraction for him. The gushing fountain of the waters of life flowing forth from the foot of the Rock of Ages lost its sparkle and freshness in his eyes. Like a balloon cut loose from its moorings he soon mounted to a dizzy height, and grew dizzy as he mounted. Nothing but the strong hand of a faithful Saviour kept him from tottering and tumbling into perdition. God gave him the desire of his heart, but sent leanness into his soul.

At last, like the prodigal that he was, he came to himself, and all the glories of the world seemed turned into husks, as they are; and even these no man gave to him. They all eluded his grasp, poor as they were. His grandest schemes failed. His gourds were cut down. His balloon was rent, and its buoyant support, poor, empty, evanescent vanity, all escaped, letting him suddenly down into the cesspool of his own folly and madness.

He appealed to Jesus, and was lifted out of the pool. Gave himself up anew and was accepted. He was delivered from his embarrassments, and made a new start in business as well as religion. Months passed — the happiest of his life, though the soberest up to that time. The Bible was a wellspring of joy to him. Prayer, especially the prayer of the closet, like the astronomer's observatory with its telescope pointed heavenward, gave him happy and hallowed communion with the bright world above; and the house of God, to him, was as the gate of heaven.

Nevertheless, there was still a want rising more and more in his soul. The want — the sense of want from a sense of his lack of — holiness. He had not yet learned to find in Jesus, by faith, the supply of this want.

Memoirs became a delight to him, and as it proved, a wondrous blessing. The memoir of another merchant of eminence, inspired him with the hope of gaining a higher level, both in the joys and the utilities of the Christian life, gave him to see as within reach even of the care-pressed, and toil-worn business man, amongst boxes and bales, customers and notes to meet, and paper to be discounted, sharpers to unmask and risks to encounter, a life both of joy and peace in Jesus, and of Christian integrity, unswerving even in the whirlpool
and whirlwind of commercial bustle and distraction.

He determined to make it his own. The way as it appeared to him — and the only one in his view — was that of uncompromising, and universal consecration to do the will of God. To give himself and his business, and his influence, personal, social, domestic, and commercial, all up to God, and hold all as the Lord's. This he did without reserve. He did not, like Naaman the Syrian, reserve the smallest thing, but gave all up. And then expected as the result of this to receive the light and joy, and comfort, promised in the word of God, and realized by the eminent merchant whose example had moved him to take this step.

To his deep disappointment, as well as great astonishment, after days and days had passed, he found his cherished hopes unfulfilled. His peace was no greater, his self-control no greater, his communion with God no greater — the same dead level of feeling — the same impurity of motive — the same power of wrong impulse remained. And now what should he do? "Try again in the same way," he thought. It did not once occur to him to ask, "Is this process of consecration all? Is there not something besides this?"

Perhaps — if it had occurred to him, and he had asked and asked at the lips of the Holy One of Israel, it might have been shown to him — that another thing was needed as much as consecration to do the will of God, viz: faith in Jesus, for the power of Him who worketh in us, to work in Him, both to will and to do of his own good pleasure. He did not ask, however.

So again he gave himself up anew to Christ, to do all his will, after surveying the past and the present and the future more carefully and solemnly than before. But the result was failure again, and again, and again, until wearied with repeated efforts, and discouraged by constant failures, he was driven to the conviction that something else must be required than consecration alone. Happily the Lord who is wonderful in counsel and excellent in working, sent him a messenger with the message —- "Believe in the Lord Jesus! It is faith in Christ you lack." He was convinced.

Then soon came another messenger and message — unseen and unheard, save in the heart of the bewildered and struggling one. But it was effectual there. It was Jesus saying, "Lo, I am with you always, even unto the end of the world." "I am he who purifieth his people unto himself. This work that you have so long struggled to have done on account of your consecration, is mine to do, and I will do it. Believe, only believe in me and it shall be done."

That was the hour and that the moment of joyful deliverance to the struggling merchant.

Many a struggle in the race of business, had been his, but never a harder one than this in the Christian race. And many a success had crowned his struggles with joy, but never one in business, or even in religion, so fruitful of happiness or usefulness as this. It was a wider and deeper opening of the channel of commerce between his soul and the mart of pearls above price, and it was the era of a revival, or rather of an enlargement of a life-long commerce, to be consummated at last by his removal to the fountainhead of that commerce itself.

Now the one point of especial interest, of this illustration in the present case, is the necessity shown by it of the faith that takes Christ as he is offered to the soul, as the Saviour from sin, just as the case of the distinguished lady given before shows the necessity of the faith that gives the soul to Jesus a living sacrifice to do all he requires.

Let either element of faith be lacking, and the soul will be like a boat with one side oar, which goes round and round but makes no progress, only drifts with the stream whirling as its drifts. Or like a bird with a broken wing, whirling over and over and falling as it whirls.

"Verily, I say unto you, except ye be converted and become as little children," says our Saviour, "ye shall not enter into the kingdom of Heaven."

The child is both obedient and docile. His father commands and he knows it is right to obey, and trusts entirely in his father's judgment and integrity, doing at once what his father bids, even when he knows nothing at all of the reasons for the command.

So again, his father promises, and he counts upon the fulfillment of the promise with the most implicit Confidence.

His father states some fact or lays down some principle, he believes it at once, and acts as if it was true.

And this is our Divine Master's illustration of the faith which opens the gates of heaven to the soul — it must be both obedient and trustful.

Chapter Three - Stopped In The Way

BY WHAT

It has been the Lord's way all along, to arrest the careless journeyer to the eternal world, at some point in his career, by some burning bush at the wayside, and then when turned aside to inquire about the matter, to press upon him the duties and privileges of the service of God.

And all along when so arrested and urged to take up the cross, it has been man's way, to conjure up a host of difficulties, as formidable as Pharaoh and his army to Moses; difficulties to be put down only by Him who convinced and persuaded Moses by the leprous hand and the changing serpent rod.

And what is true of the careless journeyer in reference to conversion, is equally true of the Christian pilgrim in reference to the second and deeper work of grace.

Indeed it often happens that it takes more to arrest and convince, in the second than in the first instance.

Abraham made his entrance upon the land of promise by two stages, first from Ur to Haran, and then from Haran to Canaan. Doubtless it cost many a sacrifice hard to make, and the sundering of many a tie hard to break, at the first, when with his father he left the land of his birth and the home of his youth, idolatrous though it was, to go forth into a strange land amongst strangers. But when, after the death of his father, at Haran, the command of the Lord came to strike tent and go forth again, he knew not where, he had no father to lean upon, no dependence but God alone, and although his faith did not fail, yet doubtless the second command tried it more than the first.

The second is the higher stage, and more difficult too. It is really harder to overcome sin in the heart, than to break away from the world at first. And it is harder to come to the point of trusting in Jesus to subdue one's own heart entirely to himself, than to venture upon him for the forgiveness of sin. We are slower to perceive that the work of saving us from sin — of expelling sin from us — is Christ's, than to see that he has already suffered the penalty of sin and purchased our pardon.

The children of Israel braved the Red Sea, and passed it in triumph — but the Canaanites in the land, in their armor of brass, and cities walled up to heaven, appalled them, and turned them back into the wilderness to wander forty long years, before they were prepared to set foot upon the land of promise.

Like them we have the two stages, and the two works, and both by faith, and both to learn.

They got not their inheritance by crossing the Red Sea alone. The Jordan must also be passed by faith between watery walls on either hand, before they could learn the lesson that by faith, they were to conquer their foes in the land, as well as gain deliverance from foes in Egypt. A hard lesson as it proved in their case, and many another. They were not stopped by the Red Sea, and they had their song of triumph upon the far bank overlooking the waters whose walls had opened to give them a dry passage, but closed upon their enemies and overwhelmed them. But when, in that same year, they came to the borders of Canaan and sent out their spies to view the land, and when the spies returned with their Eschol grapes, borne upon a pole between two of them, but reported giants, the sons of Anak in the land, and cities with walls great and exceeding high, they saw all through the magnifying glass of fear and were palsied: difficulties rose up and swelled out into the giant proportions of absolute impossibilities, and they turned from them and set their faces to go back into Egypt, and were about to murder Moses and Aaron. Nothing kept them from it but the terrible judgments of God.

Strange that they could not see, and know that the same hand that opened up
the way out of the bondage of Egypt through the Red Sea and through the wilderness, could and would open up the way into the land of Canaan and subdue all their enemies under them. "The Sea," thought they, "God opened — none but God could do that. But to conquer and subdue the land is our work, and we are not able to do it." So they shrunk back from it.

Just so it is with us. We break from the bondage of the world. We fly to the Saviour for pardon and find it. We are happy in it — we have our song of triumph after the passage of the sea, and we go forward. Bitter waters are made sweet for us by the branch of the tree of life cast in. Manna is given us to feast upon by the way. The Rock gives us its living waters. The pillar of cloud and the pillar of fire guide us all our journey through. But by and by the Canaanites in the heart begin to be seen and felt in their power. And when we begin seriously to think of their absolute subjection — we think of it as a work to be done by us — not the Lord, and we shrink back from it as hopeless, and content ourselves as well as we can with a life-long career of wandering in the wilderness, simply because our faith fails us to strike for victory, trusting in God alone to give it.

In this way multitudes are stopped, almost before they have started: just when they have come to see the land before them, but have not yet taken the first decisive step for its possession.

Already in endeavoring to take up the "stumbling stone" of perfectionism, one of the difficulties has been anticipated and answered: and in meeting the special personal plea, "not for me," another has been sufficiently discussed, if not effectually removed.

Others yet remain. God help us to see them, and conquer them too. Satan will hinder if he can.

Fear of the brand, is one great difficulty. Not merely the brand of "perfectionism" — this aside — we shrink from being marked as peculiar amongst Christians. We should not certainly greatly fear to wear the star of an earthly nobility, in some countries at least, but the star of nobility or knighthood in the army of Jesus is another thing.

Havelock fought three battles against terrible odds to gain his first honors from the Queen. But they were not his severest struggles nor his greatest victories. Many more he fought afterwards before he forced his way at last into Lucknow, but these were not his hardest contests either. The two battles with his three-fold foe, the

world, his own heart, and Satan, the first on the General Kyd, and the last at Fort William were the most trying of his life. Especially the last, when he put on the whole armor of salvation, and determined to "stand up for Jesus," even though it should cost him the loss of all favor and friendship and promotion from the crown. To be branded a "saint" was another and a very different honor to look to, than to have the star of knighthood upon his breast, and the title, "Sir Henry, K. C. B.," prefixed and suffixed
to his name.

But so it is. This battle must be fought, and he who conquers in it, comes to be willing to wear whatever title of reproach the world may see fit to confer. There is no victory without it.

Fear of becoming ultra. The danger of being led into fanaticism and error is another difficulty at the outset. And there is danger of this. Satan delights in nothing so much, if we will go forward, as to mislead us, or urge us on over the bounds of truth and wisdom out into the fields of extravagance and folly. Then, too, though old to the Bible, and to the experience of those who have gone before us, every step of real progress is new to us. We are blind to all before us, however clearly we see the ground already passed over, and our subtle enemy is always ready to decoy us into the specious network of some trap set for the unwary.

We cannot, therefore, be too careful. The fear is a wholesome one, for the danger is real. We are not without melancholy warnings in the many cases of those who have been duped in this way, and destroyed to all usefulness in this world. The following instance of...

A SHAKERESS

...is one of many like it in every essential respect, and a sad illustration of the danger in question.

She was no ordinary woman. Before she began the course which ended in her being buried alive in that Protestant American convent, a Shaker community, she was very discreet, very conscientious, very amiable, very everything apparently lovely and good. If not, like Anna, a widow of fourscore, she was yet a widow, and the widow of a respectable clergyman, with a circle of children and grand-children and friends around her, who loved and revered her. Of all women almost she seemed least in danger of being carried away from solid Scripture moorings out into the sea of fanaticism. Yet so it was. She had her weak side; there was a broad streak of the imaginative in her; charming when it was kept in subjection to truth, but inclining her to fanciful applications of the word of God. She revered the Scriptures, and any idea, no matter how absurd, if yet it suited her own fancy, and was also couched in the words of the Bible, she received as God's truth. She seemed to have forgotten that the devil can quote Scripture to his purpose. And this, her weakness, the tempter, who even tried the Master in the same way, was not slow to take advantage of. The specious and fanciful interpretation of the Scriptures by the Millerites was the first to mislead her. She went so far as to prepare ascension robes, and await the moment of the Saviour's second coming upon the day fixed by the leader, Miller, himself. Then next she was induced to come out and denounce as deluded all who did not receive the Millerite interpretation of the Bible; and that as she supposed by the direct command of God. At a certain time, while meditating upon these things, the words "Come out of Babylon" sounded in her ears, and she settled it in a moment that it was the voice of God, commanding her to separate herself from her church, amongst whom were her own beloved children and the dearest friends she had in the world; and she came out and denounced them all. After that again she was struck by the words, "Mortify the flesh," and from this she, with the little band of deluded ones whom she joined took up the idea that all they could do to mortify themselves before each other would be pleasing to God and purifying to themselves. And they carried the matter to the absurd and ridiculous extreme of placing themselves in all sorts of grotesque positions, or worse, in their meetings for worship. This finally went so far as to shock her delicacy, and drive her to renounce these Millerites in turn. And what now? Adrift once more, did she not see her folly and turn again to the stronghold? No. But went further and fared worse than ever. Meeting on board one of the lake steamers, while crossing Lake Erie, a Shakeress, her fantastic dress and demure looks attracted her, and they soon fell into conversation. Many of the fancies of this Protestant nun found admiring reception from the widow. But of all others the assurance that all the faithful have each some one of their own dear departed relatives to go with them as guardian angels delighted her most. And when her new friend said, "Does not the apostle ask, 'are they not all ministering spirits sent forth to minister to them that shall be heirs of salvation?'" the truth of all was sealed and certain to the widow's belief, as if it had been a voice from heaven, instead of the Shakeress, speaking. She was fairly caught again. The net was of gossamer texture, but yet strong enough to bind her and hold her. The Shakeress drew her out to speak of her past history and of her departed friends, and soon learned that of all the loved ones she had been called to mourn, not one, not even her husband, was so dear to her memory as a favorite sister who had been dead many years. Adroitly and demurely enough, after a while the Shakeress told the widow that her own guardian spirit, who was constantly with her had whispered that the favorite sister would henceforth attend the widow wherever she went, if she would listen to her voice in her heart and follow her counsels; and then left her to commune with her invisible attendant. Not, however, until she had taken good care to find out how much the widow was worth, and present before her in the most attractive form the question of taking all and going to the Shakers.

Left to herself, she set herself to listen to the angel voice of her invisible sister. Shall I sell all; break up, leave my children and grand-children and go? was the question silently asked. The answer as silently given was, If a man forsake not all that he hath he cannot be my disciple. If any one hate not father and mother and sister and brother he cannot be my disciple. Her fertile fancy at once took this as infallible counsel to sell all, take all and leave all and take the Shaker veil. Which she did.

Now it is in ways like this, that satan draws from the church the volunteer recruits, to keep that right wing of his army, the Fanatics filled up. With instances like this, and worse, around us, we do well to take heed. Let us beware first of all of taking impulse, or suggestions, or the inner light for our guide. Let us bring our own impulses and suggestions to the test of God's holy word. The inner light if it be not according to the revealed truth of God is only darkness. And if the light within us be darkness how great is that darkness. The mariner will hardly be so foolish as to supersede the chart, by following his own fancies upon the sea. If he should, however, some rock or shoal or reef or whirlpool would bring him up while he was sailing in fancied security and scatter his hopes and his cargo and the fragments of his ship with his crew and himself upon the raging waves of the deep. Satan has that man fairly in his snares, whom he can get to put his own suggestions or impulses, under any name whatever, whether of the inner light, or a guardian spirit or the Spirit of God in place of the Bible as the chart of faith and of life.

Let us make sure also that we have the Bible truth and not merely Bible words. It is a favorite and frequent thing with the arch deceiver to couch his own lies in words of the Scripture. He takes out and leaves behind the kernels of truth and catches the unwary with the empty chaff of mere Scripture phraseology. Beware of him.

But then, if common sense and common prudence do demand of us care lest we be deceived and ensnared, are we therefore to be stopped at the threshold of all that is good and great? No.

Rather let us be sure we are right, and then with our face as a flint, yet with the docility of the child, and with the firm tread of a mind made up and a faith leaning upon God, let us push resolutely forward to the conquest. There is just one thing that satan likes better than to lure us into fanaticism, and that is to frighten us back from any great step of real advancement into the wilderness of doubt, and the tortuous paths of unbelief and sin.

Many are stopped at the outset, by reluctance to give the world entirely up, and be wholly conformed to the will of Christ.

A moderate, reasonable, half and half life in the service of the Master they are willing to live. But to be wholly consecrated to God is more than they can consent to.

Perhaps they find the yoke of Christ heavy and galling to their necks, even when borne only in this their half and half sort of a way. And they reason by the arithmetic of unbelief which tells them that, if half and half service is all they can carry, then full service would be twice as heavy and would break them down altogether.

They fail to see that the Master gives grace and strength to those who are wholly given up to him, to "mount up as on eagles' wings, and to run without weariness, and walk without fainting."

They overlook the lessons of the past, that the Lord is the strength of those who lean wholly upon him, enabling them to pass through floods dry shod, and through fire seven times heated unscathed, to turn trials into joys, and even martyr flames into triumphs. While those who stop half way, in his service, are left with enemies around them unsubdued, unexpelled, ready to rise up and scourge them, whenever the Lord chooses to let it be done — to humble them in the dust.

Suppose a husbandman, finding his fields over-run with the noxious "Canada thistle," should, instead of waging a war of extermination, and destroying it root and branch, only make half and half work of it, should cut down part, and leave part to ripen seed and give to the winds for another crop, and so on and on from year to year.

And suppose he should justify himself to himself in this matter, by reasoning, that if it cost so much time and toil to keep the noxious things under from year to year, when all he attempted was only to keep them decently under, it would be more than he could do, if he should make the attempt, to keep them exterminated.

Such a farmer would make himself the laughingstock of the whole countryside. They would give him the title of "Canada Thistle" Smith or Johnson, or whatever his name might be. And many a homely hearty joke would be made at his expense.

But his reasoning would be — no better it is true — but just as good as that of the half and half disciple, who shrinks from whole souled consecration, because he thinks it would be so much harder than the half and half life he now lives.

But there are those who, though once willing, are now unwilling to be wholly given up to the service of Christ, hard or easy. They have not yet got enough of the world, though once they thought they had. The world has its charms for them which they are not willing to forego. Its bloom is not all shed. True they have enlisted under the banner of Christ, and in the hour of need they stand ready for the battle. They work manfully in revivals, and keep up the daily drill of closet and family worship, and the weekly duties of the sanctuary, and Sabbath school, and prayer meeting. And yet, after all; they are a sort of militia, not regulars; a citizen soldiery, ready to volunteer or be called out on occasion. Having arms and uniform hung up ready for use, but only put on and used when the occasion requires. And between whiles, attending to their citizen avocations as men of the world. And not willing at all to leave all, forsake kindred, and home, and business and all; or rather to consecrate all to the Lord, and make all subservient to the interests of his cause.

Upon such, argument will be lost. Let them take their course. They will learn by and by that Christ is made of God unto us wisdom, as well as righteousness. And that the world is folly and madness to all its votaries. Bitter in the mouth will it be to them, if at last God shall be obliged to cut down their gourds, and dash the cup of worldly pleasure from their hand.

These aside — there is another class, nearly allied to those named already before these last, to be mentioned.

Those who would gladly give themselves wholly up to Christ, but are stopped at the threshold by false or distorted ideas of what a life of entire consecration to God is.

They have the view of it which has led hundreds of thousands to go into convents and monasteries. The idea that to serve God entirely, business must be abandoned for some sort of religious occupation. But a glance will unmask this deception. A glance will serve to show that there are thousands who are engaged in religious occupations who are not wholly consecrated to God. Some, alas, who are not Christians at all. While amongst the holiest people of the world there are some soldiers, some sailors, some merchants, some lawyers, some physicians, some mechanics, some wives, mothers, house-keepers.

The truth is, a man may preach for himself to get a living or gain a reputation, just as easily as a lawyer can plead for his fees or his fame. And a merchant can make money for his Master, or a house-keeper meet her daily duties for the Lord just as well as a minister can study and teach for him.

Or they have taken up the notion that to be wholly consecrated, they must dress peculiarly — never smile — never make others smile — must wear a sanctified look, and speak in a sanctified tone, and all that. Satan helps on these distorted views of consecration.

And there is one of the wise and good counsels of our Saviour that the adversary loves to pervert for this purpose — "Count the cost." "Yes," says Satan, "Count the cost. Look the whole ground over. Take everything into view. Sum it all up. Lest haply having begun to build you shall not be able to finish, and lest having engaged in the battle you shall be put to the route."

The arithmetic he would have us use in counting the cost, is not that of figures. which cannot lie, but of fictions which cannot speak the truth. He would have us add together sacrifices, never demanded; duties, never required; and difficulties, never existing, into a fabulous sum, entirely too great for our resources to compass.

It would be useless for satan to ply us Protestants with the peculiarities urged upon Romanists. We could not be driven into petticoats, dignified as robes; nor to imprison ourselves in dungeons, called convents; nor to count beads, and call it prayers; nor to lash our own bare backs, thinking to scourge away sin. He plies us with notions more protestant, but not one whit less fictitious and deceptive. "Would you be a whole souled disciple of Christ," he says,

"Your person: — You will have to conform all your personal.habits to a rigid rule first of all. You must put on the straight jacket of propriety tight-laced. It would ill become one wholly consecrated to God to wear ornaments or elegancies. Gold and jewelry and costly array must be wholly eschewed. Luxuries of the table must never be touched; superfluities, like tea and coffee, and everything else but the coarsest fare must be let alone, or rather denounced as a wicked waste of money.

Your reading must be solidly and only religious. Your associates must be Christians only, and those the best. Your conversation should never be gay. Your face should be solemn and your words measured. You should never smile yourself or cause others to do it. Every garment, every movement, every word, every tone of your voice, should tell all around you that you are holy in no common degree.

Then as to your home: carpets and curtains, parlor ornaments and table elegancies would ill become one who professes to be wholly given up to the Lord.

Bare floors, hard chairs, plain tables and mirrors, no pictures or expensive works of art, no elegant books, no costly comforts, but everything the plainest and cheapest would better suit your professions. It would never do for you to own fine carriages and splendid horses, or spend money and time in ornamenting your grounds.

And as to your church: You would have to see to it that minister and people should come up to your standard. Rebuke them, privately first, if they did not. Rebuke them publicly afterward, if they should not heed you at first. And, if still obdurate, denounce them and .leave them. Exclude them from your fellowship. Testify against them in action as well as in words, and, if need be, set up on your own account, all alone, a church by yourself, and let the world have the benefit at least of the example of one who would have no fellowship with the works of darkness."

So he goes on from church relations to charities representing the demands of the gospel as oppressive and impoverishing in the extreme; and from charities to business, making it out an impossibility to pursue any ordinary avocation upon strictly Christian principles: and from business to politics and from politics to social life, adding absurdity to impossibility, endlessly almost. It would be tedious to follow the arch arithmetician of lies in his sum of addition. It is enough to say that he never stops until he has thoroughly frightened the half-hearted disciple back from any attempt at compliance; or if determined to go ahead blindfold, has led him on into a sea of troubles, where he must perish, if the Master does not stretch forth his hand and save him.

It will be observed that this application of our Saviour's counsel to count the cost is a complete perversion. There is nowhere in the Bible one single line or precept of rigid requirement binding the Christian to any rigid rules about living and dress, or anything of the sort. Much less a single word, making such things a condition of salvation, whether of justification or sanctification. Christ is the free gift of God to sinners, and all who believe in him really and truly will be saved, whether arrayed like Solomon in his glory in purple and gold, or like John the Baptist in a coarse garment, with a heathen girdle; and whether, like Solomon, living in palaces of marble upon the delicacies of every clime, amid the spicery of the south and the jewels of the east, and the splendors of pencil and chisel, or living in a cave in the wilderness upon locusts and wild honey, as did the greatest of all the prophets.

The kingdom of God is not in meat and drinks, nor in broadcloth and satins, or plate and perfumery and jewels, nor in the absence of these things.

The truth is, that we are never really, entirely the Lord's freemen, until we are free from the trammels of all these trivial questions, and at full liberty to follow the Lord in whatever dress or position or business or company or circumstances the providence of God and our own judgment of proprieties and our own ability and taste may dictate or require.

One class more, and the last demanding notice, of those who are stopped at the outset, may be mentioned. There are some — many it may be — who would gladly follow the Lord wholly, like Joshua, and who have just views of what it is to be given up entirely to him, but who see not how they can be sustained in entire consecration, if they make it. They do not see the hand of God out-stretched to lift them up, and sustain them; and they dare not trust to his promise, and therefore they are afraid to start.

In some respects they are like Peter in the prison at Jerusalem. They are in bondage to sin, at least, as he was to the Romans; and they know it. Their chains they have felt binding them to the world, as he felt his binding him to the soldiers by either arm. Their prison-house of darkness, with its iron gate and mail-clad watcher, has enclosed them. And a hundred difficulties in armor of brass and arms of steel, like the four quaternions of soldiers shut them in.

In this situation the gospel comes to them as the angel of the Lord came to Peter, while he slept between his keepers — and arouses them, saying, Arise, gird thyself and follow me.

But now comes a contrast.

The apostle arose, put on his sandals, begirt himself and followed, almost as in a dream. But they sit half up, in chains still, and say, "O these chains — how are they to be broken off? And the soldiers on either side — who shall free me from their weapons — and the iron gate, with its iron doors, bolts and bars, and mail-clad watchers outside, and the hundred soldiers, and the great iron gate leading to the city, and the darkness of the way?" Alas for them. The difficulties in the way appall and palsy them. If they would but arise at the call of the gospel, give themselves up implicitly and entirely to follow the Lord Jesus, he would go with them, and the way would open up in the light of his presence, and every enemy would sleep on, every barrier would swing wide open, all would go easy and delightfully. The whole way would be a way of happiness, and all the path a path of peace.

Chapter Four - The Way Missed

BY WHOM? AND HOW?

THE WAY HAS BEEN CAST UP, A HIGHWAY. HILLS DIGGED DOWN, VALLEYS FILLED UP, TO THE LEVEL OF AN EASY GRADE. STONES GATHERED OUT — THE WHOLE MADE PLAIN, CLEAR, OPEN. A CHILD MIGHT SEE IT. AND THE WAYFARER, THOUGH A FOOL, NEED NOT MISS IT.

The Lord Jesus Christ is the way. Christ all in all. Christ our justification, Christ our sanctification, Christ our glorification — He is the way.

And trust in Christ — the trust which accepts and obeys the commands, and which believes and receives the promises, is the means.

He who takes Christ for all, has all, and having all, has the peace of God passing all understanding, for he has the very God of peace with him and within him, to free him from fear, deliver him from danger, and support him in trial. With the Apostle Paul, he knows by happy experience, that "there is now no condemnation to them that are in Christ Jesus. Who walk not after the flesh but after the Spirit. For the law (power and rule) of the spirit of life, has made them free from the law (power and rule) of sin and death."

Examples, such as those of the patriarchs, and prophets, who trusted in Jehovah, (Jesus,) and the apostles and martyrs, and Luther, D'Aubigne, Baxter, Taylor, the Wesleys and Havelock, Who trusted in Jesus, (Jehovah,) mark the way as an illustrious line of journeyers in it, and as a glorious cloud of witnesses for it.

Still, however, it is so, that honest, earnest pilgrims, seeking for it, often miss it, and for a time struggle in vain to find it. True they do find it at last, and pursue it with all the greater joy for having groped for it in darkness for awhile, like the blind.

But why is it that they miss it, and how? The answer is easy for the initiated to give, but not so easy for the uninitiated to receive. It is not difficult for one who himself has missed the way and afterwards found it, to spread upon paper a chart, both of the by-ways, and also of the highway. But it is quite another affair to give eyes to the blind wanderer in any one of the by-ways to see the highway and enter into it. This indeed it is the Lord's to do, not the writer's. And he is able to do it. Let us trust him.

Before attempting to map out any of these by-ways, it may be well to point out the cause why so many take them, and so pertinaciously keep them, when the highway is so plain. It is this – a lack of docility.

Let any one who is convinced, go directly to the Lord without conferring with flesh and blood, ink and paper; stretch forth the hand of blind helplessness, to be grasped by the hand of a seeing power, and say, O Lord, lead me — and he will soon be led into the way.

Let him lay aside all his own preconceived notions, and in the spirit of the stricken Saul, prostrate on the Damascus road, let him cry, "Lord, what wilt thou have me to do?" and like Saul await the answer. And then let him obey it, and then ask again — Lord, what more must I do? and again wait the answer. And when it comes, obey that. And then again ask — Lord, what more yet? and do that, and so on. And there is no risk of presumption in saying, that in less time than the three days of groping and fasting allotted to Saul the last answer will come and the last thing be done, the struggle will end, the scales will fall from his eyes, and the light break in upon his soul.

One of three things, these wandering, struggling ones do, instead of taking the course here indicated, they either settle firmly upon some preconceived process of their own, and pursue it until scourged out of it by disappointment after disappointment; or they go to books or men for directions in stead of going directly, first of all, to the Lord, and casting all upon him; or else if they do go first to the Lord, and look to him to map out the way for them, and put them in it, they fail because they stop after the first answer, taking the first requisition for all, when it is only the beginning whereas they should keep on asking, until they see and know for themselves that they are now in the way, and have no more need to ask for the way, but only to go forward, leaning upon the arm that has led them into it.

Another sketch from life will best illustrate this. A sketch from the experience of...

A YOUNG CHRISTIAN

She was only a lamb of the flock. Young and newly converted. A few months after her conversion, the Good Shepherd drew her out and away from the world, to lead her more fully into the riches and knowledge and love of God. As he led Moses with the flock of Jethro his father-in-law into the back side of the desert to the mount of God, and there manifested himself to him under his new name, the I AM; so he led this young disciple, by the love she bore to one whom she had recently married, out upon the borders of civilization, and there in her new wilderness home, he came to her in all the brightness of the burning bush, and in all the fulness of his love.

The evidence that convinced her was too clear to be rejected, and the experience too precious to be neglected. And in the same hour that she was convinced of its reality, her resolution was taken, by the grace of God, to find the way and walk in it. And in that same hour she began asking the way, and found it.

It was a struggle. The world had wonderful attractions for her. She herself was as bright as a May morning, and as fresh and fair, and the world was as bright to her as she was to the world. Like the broad prairies around her new home, the world to her was a garden of flowers, and to all around her she was one of the most attractive of all in the whole blooming wilderness. It was therefore no slight sacrifice when the world was laid anew, and more fully than ever, on the altar again. To leave her friends and her home in the heart of the great world, and go out into a country wild and strange, was a trial which brought many a sigh from her heart, and many a tear to her cheek; but to give up the world and turn her back upon its vanities and pleasures, and devote herself entirely and forever to God, was a far greater sacrifice, even if it did not cost as many sighs and tears.

The brand, she knew would be applied, for the world never spares those who turn their back fairly upon it.

The loss of pleasures, by no means drained to the dregs, she could not but feel keenly.

To give up her own will and her own way, for the Lord's in the new and higher relations, was a submission not easy to make.

But hardest of all it was, really to believe that the Lord Jesus would do all for her that she needed and to leave it entirely with him to do, and then rest satisfied.

Moses doubtless served the Lord cheerfully and easily, as the shepherd of the flock of his father-in-law in the land of Midian, and found it easy to believe the Lord would keep him and his flock from the wild beasts and Arabs, but to follow the Lord and trust him in the new and higher sphere, as leader of Israel, to which the Lord called him from Horeb, required a higher consecration and a greater faith than he had before.

So with this young Christian, called to a higher and a holier Christian life. But as in the case of Moses, so in hers, the communion of the one hour with the Lord himself, gave the happy result, which others, who take another course than that of going directly to the Lord and looking in childlike simplicity to him to put them in the way, reach only after months and years of fruitless toil and many sad failures.

She was alone in her new home when convinced. It was one Sabbath morning. The blessed privilege of worship with the people of God, prized when she enjoyed it, and now doubly prized when host — was denied her. To make herself the best possible amends, she took to reading, prayer, and meditation.

Thus engaged the Lord met her and opened her eyes to see what great things he had yet in store for her if she would give herself up anew to him and accept of his promises.

The moment she was convinced she laid aside her book, and bowed upon her knees before the Lord and confessed her convictions, and asked what she must do. To this the suggestion came, "Give the world wholly up." This, of course, she had done already before at her conversion, as far as she then understood; but as yet, then, she did not know all the world, nor yet all of her own heart. But now she counted the cost as to pleasure and dress, and friends, and everything, and then most heartily responded, "Yes, Lord, I will." And then she asked again "What more must I do?" In answer to this came the suggestion, "You must confess all the Lord does for you before the church and the world." There was a circle around her, and a set of circumstances which made this a great trial. But again she responded heartily, "Yes, Lord, I will." And then asked yet again, "What more, O Lord?" And now came the suggestion, hardest of all. "Believe, only believe." She said "It is a great thing to believe that the Lord can and will cleanse me from all sin, and keep me by his Power, and present me spotless before the throne. He never yet has, in the past delivered me from the power of the enemy entirely. Yet I know he is almighty and I will trust him. I will believe. I do believe." This settled, she asked again, "What more, O Lord?" To which the final suggestion came, "Nothing more. This is all." It was almost as hard to believe that this was all, as to believe that Christ would do all, but she did believe and was satisfied; so she thanked the Lord for his wonderful condescension and love, and rose from her knees at rest and in peace, with new light in her heart, and new light on her pathway. The hour ended, and when the clock told out that she was entering upon the next hour, she was as truly in the highway as if she had first tried every by-way of them all, and spent months and years in weary wanderings.

Now it will be said, she was a child and easily led. That is just what I say. She was a child, and childlike she never once thought of devising any way of her own, and as for church or minister she had none to inquire of, and her book even, she laid aside, and went directly to the Lord himself, and he put her at once in the way, as he always does those who go to him in this child like spirit of dependence and teachable helplessness.

Some miss the way by taking some preconceived way of their own. A peculiar instance of this sort occurred in the case of S—— a theological student, whose habits, character and experience all justify his being called...

THE WORKER

His fellow-students and the faculty, the seminary social circle, and all the churches in the region, knew S. as the worker of the seminary. They had their lazy ones — most institutions have — and their students, par excellence, and their praying and their talking ones. S. was the worker. If tracts were to be distributed, or a religious visitation to be undertaken, or any other work to be done around the institution, S. must be one of the party, if not the sole one to do the work. If any city churches needed a worker, and called either of the professors to mention some suitable person, S. was sure to be named. If a meeting of days was about to be undertaken, anywhere in the region, whoever might be the preachers, S. was sure to be the worker.

For this all his early training on a farm, where morning, noon, and night he was at work, in seed-time and harvest, winter and summer, had fitted him physically — strong and well, he was able to work and to endure.

His conversion and religious training, had confirmed him and developed his bias, as a worker.

Young when led to engage in the service of God his activities from the first were called out in the work of his church, and his conscience was continually driving him up to do more and yet more, as his fellow-students had abundant occasion to know, for, mingled with his frequent confessions, in their meetings, of his own shortcomings in the work of the Lord, there were lashings, not few nor far apart, nor light upon the galled backs of his wincing companions, for their indolence and inactivity. Like his own sawbuck and woodsaw, with which he eked out a meagre income, he was never idle when time and chance offered for work. And whoever fell into his hands must be cut and split to the required fitness for the Masters's service, or resist a resolute and faithful workman. He was no mincer.

Probably this, his habit and character, more than everything else led his pastor and church to urge upon him the question of becoming a minister, and more than anything else pressed him on into the great undertaking of eight or nine long years' preparation in the schools.

While in the seminary, in the first part of his three years' course, a circumstance happened which still more confirmed this inveterate characteristic. In one of the city churches a meeting had been commenced. S. was engaged as usual and at work with both hands full. After a few days a singular change came over him. He ceased his working, and began to mope. He seemed terribly cast down. Ministers and people saw it and wondered at it. By and by one day he went to Mr. A., a minister in whose wisdom he had the greatest confidence, and opened his heart. He had fallen into great doubt and distress about himself. "I have been at work for years trying to save others," he said, "and I fear I am myself a castaway. I see no other way than that I must be lost."

Mr. A. answered him, saying, "O my dear brother, leave all that to the Lord. He will take care of you. Just go forward blowing the ram's horn," — alluding to a sermon just preached about the fall of Jericho, and the part in it taken by the Lord himself and the part given by him to the people — "Just go forward blowing the ram's horn, and all the walls of doubt and difficulty will soon fall down before you. You will come off conqueror, and more than conqueror over all."

In an instant his mind was made up. His work was resumed. His saddened face took on its old wonted expression of resolution, and his voice was again lifted up in the old, driving, searching style and tone. Very soon, as Mr. A. had assured him it would be, his doubts disappeared and he was triumphant.

This instruction led him at the time to a practical working faith in the Lord, and delivered him from his darkness. But it led him afterwards to fly to work itself, and trust in that, as his deliverer from whatever difficulty or danger might befall him. Was he in darkness? Work was his means of getting into the light. Was he tempted? He flew to some work of mercy to put the tempter to flight. Did coldness, drowsiness, begin to creep over him? He aroused himself, put on his coat, .put on his shoes, and sallied forth to some arduous labor until his spirit was as wakeful, and his zeal as ardent as he desired. Just as he was wont, in a cold winter's day, when the fire in his room was low, and the cold came creeping over him, so that it could not be snapped off at his finger's ends by clapping his hands and swinging his arms, or stamped off by a brisk circuit time after time around his room, then instead of increasing the fire in his stove, to go out with his saw and saw-buck, and get himself all a-glow in the wood yard; just so he managed affairs in the interests and care of the heart. Work was his sovereign specific for every ill the spirit is heir to.

In this frame and habit he was, when the Lord convinced him more deeply than ever before of his guilt and pollution, and raised the great question how he was to be purified. Others around him — not a few — he saw who had been far below him in all the activities of the Christian life, now rising by virtue of a mysterious experience suddenly far above him in all the light and love and joy and peace of the Christian. And it took him aback, put him sadly about as the expressive Scotch phrase gives it.

To set anything more excellent before S. was to put him on the stretch for it. In his own mind there was not a moment's delay when once he was convinced of the realities of the experience in question. But he did not at once acknowledge it. His pride of superiority at first would not allow that. He had given his companions too many lashings for being so far below him, to be willing at once to admit to them that they were getting above him.

Of course there was not the least question about what must be done. Work was the only thing — work would be sovereign. It always had been before; it would be now. So he redoubled his energies and activities. Laid upon his shoulders greater burdens than ever — and lashed them if through weakness of the flesh they failed to bear it. Nights he studied and prayed. Days he spent abroad amongst the people at work. Failing in this process at home, he obtained leave of absence and went abroad, to attend distant meetings in progress, working as hard as Loyola, or any galley slave ever did, and with — just as much — not a whit more — success in breaking his chains, and gaining release from the power of sin.

At last he returned humbled and dispirited, and sent for a fellow-student who had been somewhat useful as the Master's servant in leading the inquiring to look to him alone for relief and release.

To his question, "What must I do?" the response was," What have you been doing?" "Working," was the substance of the answer to this. "It is trusting, not working, by which God has ordained to save sinners," was the response again. And now opened a scene such as is rare upon earth. "What!" said S., "Do you say that working to save others, will not deliver me from my own sins?" "I do — work is not the Saviour. Jesus alone can save. Works spring from faith, not faith from works." "Do you say that praying, and fasting, and reading the Bible and teaching and leading others to do so will not, under Jesus, save my soul from the power of corruption?" "I do say just that. Your own work for yourself or others can never save your soul. You are leaning upon a broken reed, to be pierced through with many sorrows. You are rejecting Jesus the only Saviour, and putting your own imperfect and polluted work in his stead — not, it is true, as your merit, but as the power by which God is to save you. Jesus alone is the Saviour, and trust alone in him is the condition upon which he saves."

The effect of this one moment's conversation was overwhelming to poor S. Every prop upon which he was leaning seemed to be suddenly stricken from under him. His footing from the firmness of the solid rock seemed, in one instant to have dissolved to the mobility of quicksand. He threw himself back in his armchair, clasped his hands over his face, and a convulsive shiver shook his manly frame from head to foot in every muscle. He grew pallid and horror-stricken. Rolled up his eye-balls convulsively, and exclaimed, hoarsely, huskily, catching for breath, like one in the agonies of sudden death, "I am sinking! — I am sinking — into hell!"

His fellow-student sat a moment confounded — in once — then most affectionately and urgently assured S., that the arms of everlasting mercy were beneath him. That he could not sink into hell, that Jesus was with him and would save him, and much more to the same purpose, but all in vain.

Constrained at last to leave S. to himself and the Saviour, he went to his own quarters, with a subdued and saddened spirit, to bear the poor fellow up before the mercy seat in the urgent sympathising petition of faith. Next morning calling early, he found S. pale but peaceful; stripped of his glorying and trusting in works, and resting now upon Jesus. Humbled, quiet, and subdued. The storm had passed by, and swept him from the quicksand of his works, but the hand that raised the storm had been stretched forth in the midst of it to grasp him, and set his feet upon the Rock of Ages forever.

He lives to work on, and work more and more wisely than ever. Revival after revival crowned his labors. But he will never again put his works in the place of Jesus, as his Saviour from sin.

This traces in lines clear and distinct on our chart, one of the by-ways — that of works for others as a means of sanctifying ourselves.

Another is that of looking to books, or men, or both, for the light of the way which God alone can give.

Another is that of taking a bold stand for stigmatized truths and unpopular reforms, as a means of humbling ourselves in the dust, and so of sanctifying ourselves to the Lord.

Another is that of increased punctiliousness in the observance of rites and ceremonies, and all the minor matters of the law. The anise-and-mint-tithing way of the Pharisees of old, and the tractarian way of the Pharisees of our own day, upon the principle that perfection, in external sanctity, will sanctify the heart.

Another is that of praying for the Holy Spirit to come and work in us some certain states of mind and heart which we imagine to be sanctification, or holiness, seeking to be made consciously holy. Praying for the Spirit and prescribing to Him His work. Whereas, when he comes it is to work according to his own good pleasure — not according to ours — and to make us conscious of our unholiness, that we may find our holiness in Christ, not in ourselves.

Now to illustrate these by-ways one by one, each by a life sketch, would be easy, and not without interest and profit, but it would require a volume almost.

There are those who have tried nearly every by-way of them all — run each out in turn to the bitter end of disappointment, before finally going to Jesus as the way. One such would give us a complete chart of them all in the single sketch of his own blunderings. Such a one is at hand.

THE PASTOR

He is no blunderer either, in other matters. Few more careful, or wise, or discreet, than. Abundant success in his pastoral work shows that. And yet he calls himself — as we shall have occasion to see in the end, in view of the long succession of blunders made in his efforts to learn the way of sanctification experimentally — a fool. How and when and where he was convinced, is not at all essential to our chart. Possibly it may have been in connexion with a very delightful work amongst the students of another of our Theological Seminaries. Such a work there was, and in it many of the young gentlemen came to see and understand the way of sanctification by faith, and to be filled with the Holy Spirit, and the pastor knew much of this work and commended it publicly. It would be a glorious thing, if from year to year, each and all of our schools of the prophets could be baptized in this way.

Possibly it was the conscious leanness of his own soul which made him hunger and thirst for the precious things of God. Not that he was not a devoted Christian and minister. There was no apparent lack of this kind. Indeed he was far more than most others a faithful, earnest, tender, thorough, pastor and preacher, and for this very reason he would be the more likely to feel deeply his own want of this very experience of the way of sanctification. Those who are most earnest in pressing forward, come soonest into the light, which reveals their own pollutions. The laggards among the prophets, are not apt to have visions of God in his exalted purity and glory making them exclaim, "Woe is me! for I am a man of unclean lips." Such a vision — with the live coal from the altar to take away our sins, would be a blessing of unspeakable value to every ambassador of Christ, and there are many who would welcome it, gladly. Perhaps it was the increasing desire to do good, and to learn the way to gain the power from God to do it. Such aspirations are indeed angel visitants — not few or far between — in the pastor's heart.

But, however it was, at the time our sketch commences, the pastor had become deeply convinced and was earnestly longing for the experience in question. He was a student, and student-like, his first resort was to books. Whatever his own library contained, or the bookstores could supply, or other libraries could lend, he got and devoured, upon the subject of the higher forms of Christian experience. He red over the memoirs and writings of the most noted in each of the three classes we have named. Lutheran," "Wesleyan," and "Oberlinian." He ranged about and fed with the greediness of Pharoah's lean kine, and gained — as much — but no more by it. He read, marked, learned, and inward-digested, the experiences of all he could hear about, who had found the way to the tree of life and fattened upon its twelve manner of fruits but he was lean as ever.

His church had reason to know something of this. If he devoured books as the silk worm does mulberry leaves, for his own food, it gave material for pulpit and the prayer meeting, which like the cocoons of the silk worm, the people had occasion to spin and weave into close fitting garments for themselves. Like others who write bitter things against themselves, he of course told his people over and over, that they were no better than they ought to be, and were in great need of a deeper work of grace as well as himself. Like Leigh Richmond under conviction, unconverted but preaching, he preached his people into convictions like his own, but had no power to point them the way out; for as yet, and for a long while, he did not know it himself.

Meanwhile, he wrote to the living, or visited them from whom he hoped to receive light. But neither the illustrious dead by their memoirs, nor the living by their words, could give him the light of the way of life. They could tell him what to do — could tell him to consecrate himself, and to believe; but they could not make him understand. The Lord alone could do that, and he had not yet learned to go as a child and ask the way.

Strange we are so slow to learn that the Lord alone can open the eyes of the blind, unstop the ears of the deaf, and set the prisoner free!

All books, like the book in the Apocalypse, are sealed, until they are opened by Him who sits upon the throne. And the living teacher, though he were an Isaiah, is no better than the dumb, until our ears are opened by the Lord to hear, and our heart to understand his words. The word of God itself is only a dead letter to us, until we look to the living Saviour for light, and he then makes it a quickening spirit.

The pastor failed to look to Jesus directly for the light and so every book from the Bible downwards failed to give it to him.

Baffled in this quarter he turned to another. His next movement was that of humbling himself by taking a bold stand for unpopular truths and reforms. Pulpit and platform and press, groaned under his appeals. He challenged the world to say what it pleased about him, and let them know that he was not to be turned from his course, or kept back by fear of the brand. Relentlessly and heroically he pushed his crusades. Not so much, however, in hope to secure the reforms, as to humble and sanctify himself. And what was the result? Was he humbled and sanctified? No. But lifted up in the pride of his heart, so that he began to despise his brethren who did not come out and stand with him, and stand by him; and although not at all inclined to censoriousness, it was hard for him to withhold denunciations of their course. At last — seeing as he did, the rising pride of his heart, when he looked to see it thoroughly humbled in the dust — hope from this quarter died out and he turned to another.

It would have been strange indeed, if he had not tried making the outside of the cup and the platter clean, to sanctify the inside. He did not indeed pull up his carpets, and sell them, with every other elegance or curiosity or luxury of his house, as some have done. His tasteful and excellent wife, might have put in some serious objections if he had proposed it. Possibly he thought so, and therefore said nothing to her about it. Another minister, who had gathered a splendid library, sold all and gave to the poor, under a similar pressure, reserving only a few devotional books, and a few absolutely indispensable.

Our pastor was wiser than that. He left his library complete. It seems not to have once occurred to him, that putting the light out of his library might bring it into his mind; at any rate he did not try it. The mint-and-anise process, of course, reached his wardrobe and person, though not to any very ridiculous extreme. He did not go as far as the lady who sold her wedding ring, and then disposed of the old watch, the heirloom of her paternal ancestry, because conscience would not down at her bidding, and because she hoped by stripping her person of the last jewels and ornaments, to bedeck her spirit with the higher graces coveted.

But whatever he did or did not do, he failed in all, and gave up hope in this quarter in turn.

He had now tried, first, inquiring of books and men for the way, and failed. Next, he had sought humility of heart by braving reproach, and failed. Next, he had tried punctilious observances; regulating dress and time, and occupations, and expenses, and intercourse with the world, and everything by rule, as a means of regulating the heart, and failed.

What next?

Now he turned to seek the Holy Spirit by prayer, to do the work which he took it for granted would be done; that is, cleanse his soul and give him to feel that he was really holy. This he pushed more urgently than all before. Every book upon prayer was searched, the Bible above all. Every example of the prevalence of man with his God, and every promise, was weighed with the care of one who is gathering and sifting gold dust for his bags. Not simply to be treasured either, but to be used, rather as bank-notes are by the holder who presents them at the counter for payment.

Through all his struggles and troubles, his church of course, shared largely, whether they knew it or not, what was passing in his heart. And more than ever he had come now, upon a course which was suitable to urge upon them. They were stirred up to pray, as they never had been before. Pray to test the power of prayer. Pray to sanctify themselves. Pray that the Lord would come down and work in pentecostal power in their own hearts and in all around them. And they did pray — but their pastor prayed more; and more than they all. Hour after hour, alone with his God, he wrestled with the pertinacity of a Jacob, but not like Jacob to prevail.

Time passed on; day after day, week after week flew by, and yet the blessing delayed. The Spirit did not come upon either pastor or people. He was confounded, and began to inquire what it could mean. He was at last completely at his wit's end and falling before the Lord confessed it. His plans, one after one, had all been tried out and failed. He could devise nothing more; now what should he do? There was nothing more that he could do but to therefore in all this history of successive struggles inquire of the Lord what to do. For the first time he was prepared to come to the Lord himself, not to have any plan of his own confirmed and carried out, but to ask after the Lord's plan, and be led into it. And this he did most heartily. He threw himself upon the Saviour to be shown the way, and there he rested the matter.

Rising from before the Lord, he opened his Bible at the oft read seventh of Romans, and read over again the history in miniature, of his own vain struggles in the weary months and years gone by. Coming to the closing question, "O wretched man that I am who shall deliver me from the body of this death?" he read it and re-read it with a sigh, and then passed on to the answer, "I thank God through Jesus Christ my Lord." The light flashed through his soul, that Jesus was the deliverer from sin, just as he had been his deliverer from condemnation. And springing to his feet he could scarce restrain himself from leaping for joy, exclaiming, "What a fool I have been! What a fool I have been! Strange I have never seen this before. There never has been an hour through all this time, when if I had seen any one doing to obtain forgiveness of sin what I have been doing to obtain purification from sin, that I should not have said, 'O foolish man, you are rejecting Christ the way in vain efforts to be saved in your own way.' What a fool I have been! What a fool I have been!"

Light came in a flood. His joy was tumultuous.

By and by, when it calmed down to something like the even flow of peace, he opened his Bible and ran it through and through, everywhere seeing the confirmation of the fact that sanctification like justification is by faith in the Lord Jesus, that the just shall live as well as be made alive by faith.

And now commenced a new era in his preaching and teaching. The days of scolding were over and gone. He had found green pastures for his flock, and he delighted to lead them there, and they were delighted to be led.

Now also came the beginning of a revival in that church, the end whereof has not yet been seen at this writing. Through all the days of scolding and driving, neither pastor nor people could do for the cause of the Redeemer what now it is easy for them to do. For now they have a mind to the work; and they work with a will and a wisdom new in their history. Many a dark place never ventured upon before, has now been lighted up by their presence, and many a hard piece of work, too hard for them in all the past, has now been undertaken and done. And so the wilderness all around is made glad for them and the desert begins to blossom as the rose.

With this sketch of the pastor's experience, we close these illustrations of the way to attain abiding union with Jesus.

In endeavoring to show what it is, a basis has been laid, in historical examples. And in illustrating the way, sketches from life have been given.

These sketches have all been drawn from the world of fact, not of fiction. Most of them are narratives of scenes and circumstances which have taken place under the writer's own observation.

In taking these, rather than those already on record, we have hoped both to secure greater interest and also to add to the wealth of the church in its treasures of this kind.

Strange and extraordinary experiences have not been sought, but rather the simple histories of the more frequent workings of God in salvation.

Strange things startle and arouse, but guidance and instruction come rather from scenes and circumstances not too far above us.

"You come down to me, in what you say. I can understand you. You make it plain and simple. Others bewilder me. They talk of things too high -- too wonderful for me. I cannot understand them."

This is a remark the successful teacher often hears. His is a work, not of dazzling, but of leading. And hitherto this has been our aim.

Passing now to the illustration of the progress and power gained by abiding in Jesus, the same course will be followed. The Bible, and Memoirs, and hitherto unrecorded facts, known to be facts, will be the staple of our material. God grant grace and wisdom in the work. To Him be glory, all the glory, and always the glory. Amen.

Part Three - Progress and Power

Chapter One - Stages of Progress

STARTING POINTS NOT STOPPING PLACES.

"I do not like this idea of a definite point to be gained. I have no faith in any stopping place in the Christian course this side of heaven."

The tone of this remark had a shade of impatience and contempt, accompanied by just the slightest curl of the lip and all the emphasis of a finality.

The young gentleman who made it had, the day before — it was now Monday morning — been trying the new-fledged wings of his recent licensure, and was just returning in the cars to the halls of theological lore, to make a new sermon or mend the old one, against the time of the next invitation from an over-worked pastor needing respite, or a vacant church, seeking supply.

The gentleman to whom it was made was one of some dozen years' experience as a minister of the gospel, seated by his side in the cars. The two had providentially met a few moments before in the depot, and been introduced by a mutual friend. Seated together, and whirling along toward B., they beat about for a while in desultory conversation upon various things general or personal, but soon settled, upon the topic of the higher walks of the Christian life. Some turn in their talk had called out this remark.

"No," added the young gentleman deliberately, with a peculiar emphasis of a deep downward inflection on the word hate. "No, I hate the idea of a certain fixed point to be gained — a resting place — the all in all to be aimed at or expected by the Christian."

His travelling companion, in the softened tone of a mellowed experience of the love of Christ, and of a developed patience with the foibles of mortals like himself, suggested that perhaps his friend had yoked together a right idea with a wrong one, and was condemning the innocent with the guilty, simply from having himself unwittingly placed it in bad company. "You are certainly right in rejecting the idea of any stopping place for the Christian this side of heaven; but are you sure that a definite point in experience is a stopping place."

"We are rushing along in the ears at the rate of twenty miles an hour towards A., and I have no thought of stopping until it is reached; but we have just now passed the very definite point B., in our journey, and have been doubly advertised of the fact by the car whistle as we were halting, and the clear voice of the conductor calling out B., in the long-drawn manner to be heard over all the din of voices and clatter of feet, and also by the name B., in large letters upon the front of the depot. And in a few moments again, we shall come to C., another very definite point — both on our checks and on the bills, known and read of all journeyers by rail. And yet beyond the moment spent in wooding and watering, and stretching our limbs — are they in any proper sense stopping places — much less the all in all aimed at and expected by journeyers to A.? Are they not — mere stages in the journey — new and nearer starting points for home? You do not believe in conversion perhaps?"

"O yes, indeed I do and teach it too. I believe in it, and urge it with all my might upon everybody as a distinct experience, the privilege and necessity of all, known by signs before and signs following, clear and easily distinguishable."

"Well, is the new birth a final stopping place?'"

"O, no, indeed! Too many, it is to be feared, think they have gained all — when once they have had clear evidence that they have been born again — until they are afterwards reluctantly taught better, but it is only the starting point of the Christian race."

"Well, may there not be another period as well, the new starting point of a higher progress, just as distinctly marked as conversion itself, and the second no more a stopping place than the first?"

The young gentleman was interested — not convinced — and eager and more eager as they rushed on toward the moment and place of separation, to have his car companion unfold his ideas of the unfolding Christian life.

Willing rather to put his young friend upon the permanent track of a higher happiness and of a nobler usefulness, than merely to gratify any momentary curiosity, the servant of Jesus graphically delineated the two stages of experience as they have been given to the world by eminent men from their own personal history, Luther and D"Aubigne amongst the number. Each stage he described as the definite attainment of an actual progress, the first as the victory conquering peace, and the second as a new start, both in a richer peace and a more expansive wisdom and beneficence.

As the conversation went on and the point of separation drew near, the fire kindled in the ingenuous heart of the young man and shone forth in his noble face.

Hope — a new hope of gaining for himself, Luther like, a deeper, stronger vital union with the True Vine, and a more generous fruitage in the vineyard of his Lord, just now opening out before him, sprang up in his soul. He frankly confessed his fruitless struggles and sad disappointments in the past, and as frankly owned his now newly awakened hope for the future. Many things said by his companion struck deep into the generous soil of his ardent young heart, and clear and active mind: nothing however more deeply than the two-fold significance of the text which became the Reformer's watchword and talisman, "The just shall live by faith." The just shall be made alive first, and afterwards learn to live by faith. The just shall be justified before God first, and afterwards learn the way to become just also in heart and life, by faith. This two-fold significance of the text, illustrated by its suggestion the first and the second times in the Reformer's heart, as by a celestial voice within, with the interval of years between the two, and meeting in each case a want so different, caused the young man to exclaim, "O the depth of the riches of the word of God! What hidden force it contains! We get but half of it at most, and then too often think we have all!"

They parted with reluctance. But cars like time and tide wait for no man. With their shrill signals and ringing-bells, they constantly reiterate the words of warning and wisdom, "What thou doest, do quickly," though, alas, only too many like Judas are hurried on by them to the betrayal of the Master for silver. Not so with our travellers, however. Our young friend had even now, got a spur arid a life-long power also in the work of his Master, and his companion's heart like the fountain, welling up and full to the brim, was all the fresher and not a whit the less full for all he had given to his thirsty fellow-traveller by the way.

Was it not just such conversations, in just such places that the prophet Malachi referred to, when he said, "Then they that feared the Lord spake often one to another, and the Lord hearkened and heard, and a book of remembrance was written before him. And they shall be mine, saith the Lord, in that day when I make up my jewels. And I will spare them as a man spareth his own son that serveth him."

Surely, the Lord, in this instance, did stoop down and bend his ear to their talk by the way, for he evidently sealed it to the permanent blessing of the young man, giving him — it may be hoped — in his own happy experience the evidence in his own case of a definite point gained, not a final stopping-place, but the new and nearer starting point of a higher and happier progress. The moment came. They had met for the first time, and now were about to part for the last time, to meet again — not until that hour when each shall come bearing his sheafs with him. Their hearts were touched; the warm grasp of their hands told it more than their words.

"I shall never forget you, sir, nor this hour in the ears. Already, long ago, I was made alive by faith, and the day and the hour are engraven in living letters in my memory. It was the starting point of Christian life with me; but never until this hour have I learned that the way to live, is also, and in the same way by faith. Now I trust God has taught it to me, and this is to me a new and is a higher stage and starting point. May God reward you, sir. Good by." "Good by. The Lord make you wise and strong to teach others the way. God bless you." So they parted, the one to go on his way to B. and the other to turn off, and return to the venerable school of the prophets.

While upon this subject of stages and starting points, there are yet two or three questions to be answered:

First: Why speak of stages in the Christian life at all. Is it not a thing of gradual growth, like the plant, from the blade to the full corn in the ear, and of steadily unfolding progress, like that of the light from the first grey dawn of the morning twilight onward to the perfect day, rather than a thing of steps and stages at all?

Here again is another mal-adjustment of ideas: Not now, however, the yoking together of two ideas not yoke-fellows at all, the one true and the other false, and so of condemning the true with false, as the young man in the cars did, but the separation of two ideas both alike true, and true yoke-fellows, and pitting them one over against the other, like David and Goliath arrayed in mortal combat.

The Christian life is, indeed, plant-like, a thing of gradual growth; but then it is also none the less plant-like as a thing of stages.

Conviction is its first stage and starting point. The truth, like the seed sown by the husbandman, may have lain long buried under the soil of youthful levity, or under the hard crust of a heart often reproved; but at last, when the rain and the sunshine of heaven come down upon it, it begins to feel the power of a divine energy within and swells and bursts its cerements of worldliness, and pushes upward, feeling after the light of heaven until it comes forth "the blade," a new creature born of God into the kingdom of light.

Conversion is a new and a higher starting point, from which plant-like the Christian life unfolds, joint after joint, leaf after leaf, stretching upward and onward for fruitage and fulness of stature, until at last it gains the fruit-bearing status of true Christian manhood and majority and liberty, and rejoices in that stage of its progress marked by our Saviour as "the corn."

Having now learned the way to live by faith, it goes on ripening its fruit for the golden harvest, and the heavenly garner of its Lord, and becomes in due time the "full corn in the ear," ready for the sickle of the angel reapers.

Or, taking the figure of the light, increasing more and more to the perfect day, you have the same two ideas of gradual growth, and yet of stages of progress, harmoniously and beautifully blended and expressed. For while the light pours in upon us, in ever increasing flood, through the opening gates of day, from the first rays gladdening night's darkest hour onward until, in noontide splendor, the day is perfected. Yet is there not first the dawn, then the sunrise, and finally the noon of the perfect day? Strange that an argument for the rejection of the idea of distinct stages in the Christian life should ever have sought its basis in these comparisons, which so beautifully and clearly express and illustrate the very ideas sought to be condemned by the argument!

The same idea is also given by the apostle Paul in his Epistle to the Romans i. 17. "For therein (in the gospel) the righteousness of God (to all and upon all that believe, Jew and Greek,) is revealed (made manifest) from faith unto faith (from stage to stage) as it is written the just shall live by faith."

And how vivid the living comment and confirmation of Luther's actual progress by stages in connection with this very text!

Expressed again also by the apostle to the Corinthians, second Epistle, iii. 18, by a figure which gives the true philosophy of the whole glorious mystery of our sanctification or transformation into the image of God by a single dash of the pen. "But we all with open face beholding as in a glass the glory of the Lord are changed into the same image from glory to glory, as by the Spirit of the Lord." That is the Holy Spirit as promised by our Lord to his disciples — takes of the relations of Christ to us, and unfolds them before us, while we behold his glory, and his glorious fitness exactly to meet each want of our souls, as in turn one after the other they unfold and press upon us, whether of justification from the law, or of sanctification to God, or of glorification in his presence above; and thus we are changed by the view of Christ into his image from glory to glory. The same thing is expressed also by the apostle in another form in first Cor. i. 30, where the various relations of Christ are unfolded in order to us as they do actually open out in experience, to meet our unfolding wants from stage to stage. "Made of God unto us WISDOM," that is conviction of folly and sin, conviction, as Jesus himself says, because they believe not on me. The fear of God which, according to King Solomon, is the beginning of wisdom — RIGHTEOUSNESS — that is, justification from sin —SANCTIFICATION — that is transformation into the likeness of God — and REDEMPTION that is transfiguration from the earthly image of the Lord to the glorious image he bears now in heaven, and translation to heaven.

The answer, therefore, to the question, "Why speak of the Christian life as a thing of stages at all? is first of all because it is so, and so to speak of it is to speak truth.

But this is not all. There is another reason impelling it, because it is a fire in the bones — it must out.

And another and a better one still, because it is the way of all ways to arrest attention, and induce men to press for the experimental apprehension of that which is set before them.

The preaching of John the Baptist had this striking feature, that it was distinct and clear above all who had gone before him, and therefore his success was greater, insomuch that the Saviour said that, amongst those born into the world a greater had not arisen than John. His trumpet had the clarion ring of an Elijah in its power. And it had also the clear ring of an apostle almost in the definiteness with which he presented the one stage of experience, "metanoia " change of heart.

The force of John's preaching is in some measure hidden to us by the translation of the word metanoia as repentance, whereas its full meaning is new birth or change of heart. But as we, in imagination, bend the ear and listen to the prophet on the banks of the Jordan, proclaiming to the gathering crowd coming from far and near, the baptism of repentance, the need of a change of heart to escape the damnation of hell, we might almost imagine it to be Whitefield on Bristol common, reiterating the Saviour' s words, "Except ye shall be born again, ye cannot see the kingdom of God," and urging his message by depicting the wrath to come. It was just this vivid apprehension of the truth, and this definite presentation of it, which gave both the Judean and the Anglican prophets such power and success.

The success of the apostles in winning men to the higher experience — the baptism of the Holy Ghost — first received by themselves, and then definitely proclaimed by them to others, as the privilege of all who would believe on the Lord Jesus, was due also, in great measure, to the definite vividness, with which they set this stage of the Christian life before men as an object of desire and attainment.

There are those who seek to muffle the arrows of truth, lest their naked points should pierce the heart and hurt the feelings, but arrows must be sharp in the hearts of the king's enemies, or they will not fall under them.

It is the lack of a definite experience, first, in our own hearts of the fact and truth that Christ is made of God unto us sanctification, and then the consequent lack of a clear and vivid presentation of it to others, as an experience within sure and easy reach of all who will make it a point, and urge their way to it which, more than everything else — love of the world not excepted — keeps the church back from receiving and living in the fullness of the blessings of the gospel of peace.

The second question is this: Admitting that the Christian life is one of stages, do all Christians pass through the same — the same in number and variety?

The answer is both yes and no. Yes, if the question embraces only such stages as are essential to: salvation. No, if it relates to such as have their occasions in the peculiar circumstances of individual life.

A glance must satisfy every disciple of Christ, that in the case of every sinner saved, unless filled with the Holy Ghost from his mother's womb like John the Baptist, there must be a period of conviction — a time when he is convinced of sin — else he never could repent and be saved.

And also the period of conversion; the moment when he does repent of sin, forsake the world, and become the Lord's; else he never would be the Lord's.

And a time likewise when he comes to the perception and reception, of the fact that Jesus will cleanse him from all sin, and fit him for heaven; else he never will be fitted for heaven, for Jesus alone can fit him, and faith alone is the condition upon which he does it.

These several periods may, or may not be marked at the moments of their occurrence, and may or may not be remembered afterwards. They may be very unequal in the intervals between — sometimes all crowded into a moment, as in the case of the thief on the cross. Sometimes the period of conviction may last a life-time almost, and the subsequent stages all be passed through in an hour, as in the case of the brother of George Whitefield, who after long years of gloomy forebodings, at last, while at the table of Lady Huntingdon, caught from her lips the words that Jesus came to seek and save that which was lost, and in these words received Jesus by faith — and next morning was dead — already washed white and made pure in the blood of the Lamb, and presented faultless by the hand of him whom he had so lately received as the seeker and Saviour of the lost. Sometimes the interval after the conviction may be only a moment before conversion, but a whole lifetime may be spent after conversion before learning that faith is the victory that overcometh; and at last, after terrible struggles and fears, like those of that wonderful man, Dr. Payson, he may in the evening hour of life learn the great secret of the gospel as the way of salvation from sin, and have a peaceful — yea, a gorgeous sunset of it.

So, also, these several periods may each be separated from every other, and from everything else, so as to be clearly and distinctly described as stages of experience, or they may be so associated with other and peculiar circumstances of individual life as to be regarded by themselves and others, as special incidents of their own peculiar lot in the world.

As for example, the case of...

A NEW ENGLAND LADY IN THE WEST

Before becoming the bride of the man of her choice, she had espoused the bridegroom of the church. Indeed, in giving to him her heart with her hand, she gave him clearly to understand that it was a heart in which Jesus was enthroned. This he liked well — for he too had settled the great question of life first of all, long before becoming engrossed with the questions and cares of a settlement in the world.

So, as they journeyed westward through the — then dense forests of the new country, they had the company of him who had proclaimed himself to Jacob at Bethel, and promised him never to leave him or forsake him until he should have done all that he had told him of. And when they threw up their log cabin, in the unbroken wilderness, and kindled their first fire on the hearth, and prepared their first repast in their new forest home, and sat down for the first time to their table spread in the wilderness for them, the cheerful blaze in the heart toward God was brighter than the fire on the hearth, and they had meat to eat which was unseen on the table — their cabin and table, and all like themselves to each other were regarded as God's gifts, and held by them as God's stewards.

But days of darkness came. Children were born to them and given to the Lord from their birth — but it was hard for them, the mother especially, to lay them in the grave. The death of their first born, with its mutiplied sorrows, and the long weary watchings induced a low long running fever from which, after many months, she recovered, but always bore the marks of it in two ways: first, in a weakened body weighed down with infirmity, and second, in a strengthened heart borne up by a trust and a peace never felt before.

Her murmurings and rebellions in the days of her trial had brought up to the surface all the deep sediment of sin, and startled her at the sight of herself, and her sickness had called up the judgment as at hand, and her own heart had condemned her as unfit and unready to meet the welcome of her Judge. She was afraid to die, but her struggles to prepare were as vain as any attempt could have been to remove mountains, until at last in sheer despair, she cast the whole care of her sins — the cure of her sins — as well as their pardon, upon Christ and was at peace. While at the same time she cast all her cares for her own health and the safety of her husband and children, and indeed every thing else on the Lord: and when at last she rose from that weary but blessed bed, she was changed to herself and to every body else. Calm and peaceful, placid and happy.

But then it was so connected in her own mind and the mind of others with the deaths of her child and her own illness, that it was always spoken of as a special result of the Lord's special chastenings upon her — altogether a special thing — while in fact, hidden under the special circumstances of her case, there was the experimental apprehension of the way of salvation from sin by faith in the Lord Jesus, which was the hidden spring of the great change in her feelings, and the open fountain of her peace and good fruits abounding in all after life.

And this brings us to the second answer — No. No, to the question, Do all Christians pass through the same stages of experience, when the question embraces such stages as are peculiar to the special mission or circumstances of particular individuals.

While there are general features of likeness amongst all, each one has his own special mission in the world, and his own special occasions with God.

Not every one like Abraham is called upon to pack up all — strike tent and away for a strange land, the very name and boundaries of which lie knows nothing at all.

Not every one like Abraham is called upon to lay an Isaac upon the altar and lift the knife to slay him, and then to hear the angel voice that commands him to stay his hand, for God had prepared himself a Lamb. Why? Because not every one is called to become the father of nations hike Abraham and the father of the faithful.

These experiences of the patriarch are peculiar to himself, because peculiar to his mission. And yet Abraham at some time and in some way, had to pass through the period of conviction, and afterwards learn the way of pardon by faith, and also of purification in the same way; all the same as any of the multitudes who call him father.

Oftentimes, doubtless, there is — in the wise providence of God a combination of that which is general with that which, is peculiar, as in the case of the Lady in the West. The Bethel scene in the life of Jacob is an instance of this kind. His peculiar distress in leaving his home and losing the heirship of his father's wealth, sold to him by Esau in the birthright for a mess of pottage, but wrested from him again by threatened violence, together with his fears for his own safety in the long lone wilderness journey before him, and his own sins rising up in accusation against him and bringing with them dread of God's wrath, caused him to cry unto God in the bitter anguish of despair, as he was about to pillow his head on the stone and stretch his weary limbs on the ground for the night.. And this made occasion for God to manifest himself to him, and unfold to him his purposes towards him, and his loving care and kindness over him. And this in turn called forth the vow of service from Jacob, and filled his heart with a joyous faith in the Lord.

Under all these specialties there was, all enfolded in their drapery, the one great generality — the youthful patriarch's conversion to God.

He went forth from Bethel a new creature, born not of man nor of the will of the flesh, but of God.

The third and last question relating to this topic of stages and starting points, is this: must all who are saved, then pass through the stage of experience called for convenience second conversion?

The answer here again is both yes and no. No, if by the question it is intended to ask whether every one or any one must have a time of deep anxiety and violent struggling, like many whose experiences have been sketched in these pages, followed by a moment when light breaks in, and joy springs up, and peace overflows, and doubt and darkness all flee away.

Any particular kind of experience is nowhere in the Bible made a pre-requisite of salvation. He who really and truly believes in the Lord Jesus, will be saved whether he has any experience at all to relate or not.

Like the record of the patriarch ISAAC'S LIFE, there may be a life laid on the altar of God, by parental faith in infancy, followed in due time by a faith in the child, like the little boy prophet Samuel's, as bright as an Abraham's and yet too early in its beginnings, and too steady in its unfoldings to be marked by memory or recounted in its stages; a life which life-long, is a living sacrifice to God, unceasingly sending up the smoke of its incense from the glowing fire in the heart, kindled and fanned and fed by the Holy One of Israel, and yet with no particular Damascus Road, or Bethel scene to mark it from first to last. And who will say that such a life is any less the living epistle of God, or any the less the sure precursor of heaven, than the life of vicissitudes and vacillations, marked by a Bethel, a Mahanaim, a Jabbok and a Shechem, like the patriarch Jacob's?

But then, on the other hand, if the questioner means to ask whether it is necessary for all to come to the point of trusting in the Lord for purity of heart to be prepared for heaven, the answer is yes. For there is no other way under heaven to be purified but by faith in the Lord. And none but the pure in heart shall see God in peace.

This may be learned sooner or later in life, and with or without a distinct period of struggling, followed by the joys of knowing the glorious truth; but it is a point that must be gained, or heaven must be lost.

Millions have lived life-long in ignorance of it, trembling often and often at the thought of death and of their own unfitness for heaven. And at last, in the very last days, or hours, or moments, or seconds of life, the glorious fact that Jesus would purify them and present them whiter than snow in is his own spotless robes has been revealed to them, and all their doubts and fears have been swallowed up in the triumphs of faith.

GOVERNOR DUNCAN

...of Illinois, is an illustration of this.

For many years the Governor was distinguished as a Christian — a consistent member of his church. A rare and a shining mark, both for the jests of ungodly politicians, and for the happy references of all lovers of Jesus.

It is a very lovely thing, and only too remarkable to see one occupying the highest position of honor in a State, himself honoring the King of kings. Happy is the people who exalt such a ruler, to the places of power, and happy such a ruler, in his exaltation, more, however, in the humility with which he bows to Jesus, than in the homage which the people pay to him.

His conversion was clear and satisfactory, and he renounced all merit of his own as the ground of his acceptance with God. The blood of Jesus, the Lamb of Calvary, was all his hope. He was firmly grounded in the atonement of Christ. And all went well until death and the judgment drew near. About three weeks before the hour of his departure, he was seized with an illness which he himself felt would end in his death. And with the premonition of death came the question of fitness for heaven. He was troubled. His unfitness was only too apparent for his peace. The fever of his mind was higher than the fever in his veins — and, alas he had not yet learned that Jesus is the physician of unfailing skill, to cure every ill that the spirit is heir to. He saw plainly enough how he could be justified from the law that it should not condemn him; for its penalty had been borne already by the Saviour himself; and its claims on the score of justice were all satisfied. But he did not see that the same hands which had been nailed to the cross would also break off the manacles of sin, wash out its stains and adjust the spotless robe of Christ's perfect righteousness upon him, and invest him with every heavenly grace.

His perplexity was great. The night thickened upon him, his soul was in agony, and his struggles utterly vain.

The point of despair is sure to he reached, sooner or later, by the struggling soul, and the point of despair to him who abandons all to Jesus is also the point of hope. The Governor at last gave over and gave up, saying in his heart, " Ah! Well. I see it is of no use. Die I must. Fit myself for heaven I cannot. O, Lord Jesus I must throw myself upon thy mercy, and die as I am."

This hopeless abandonment was the beginning of rest to his soul. Indeed, it was the victory that overcometh. Soon the loveliness of Jesus began to be unfolded to him, and he saw that the way of salvation from sin was by faith in the Saviour. The fire in his veins burned on, steadily and surely consuming the vital forces of his manly frame, but the fever of his spirit was all allayed by the copious and cooling draughts given him from the gushing fountain of the waters of life flowing from the smitten Rock, and his joy was unbounded.

As his stricken and sorrowing family gathered around his bed for the last words of the noble man, he told them with a face radiant with joy, that he had just found what was worth more to him than riches, or honors, or office, or anything else upon earth. "The way of salvation by faith in the Lord Jesus Christ," and he charged them as his dying mandate, by the love they bore him, not to rest until they too — whether already Christians as he himself long had been, or not, had also found the same blessed treasure.

They asked him what legacy he wished to leave for an absent relative, whom they knew it was his intention to have remembered in the division of his estate.

"That is all arranged in my will," said he. "But tell her from me that I have found the way of salvation by faith in the Lord Jesus Christ, and if she too will find that, she will find infinitely more than I could bestow upon her, if I should give her all I am worth in the world."

They mentioned the name of a distinguished fellow officer and special friend of the governor's, living in a distant part of the State, and asked if he had any message for him.

"Tell him that I have found the way of salvation by faith in the Lord Jesus Christ, and if he will also find it for himself it will be better than the highest offices and honors in the reach of man upon earth."

So he died. "0, had he only known this before," you say. Yes, that was just what he himself said. "0, had I only known this when I first engaged in the service of God, how happy I should have been! And how much good I could have done!"

How like the dying regret of Dr. Payson. Likening himself in the fulness of his bliss, as the chariot of fire which should bear him to heaven drew near, to a mote floating in the sunshine of infinite love. He exclaimed, "0 had I only known what I now know twenty years ago!"

And this might answer still another question should it be asked as it often has been, viz.

How does it fare with all those professors of religion who live on to the end of their days without the experimental knowledge of the way of sanctification by faith?

Badly, of course, if they are mere professors, and not truly converted, as it is to be feared too many are. For they have not been justified, and therefore they cannot be either sanctified or glorified, but will be banished from the presence of God and the glory of his power forever, and covered with shame everlasting contempt.

But, if really converted, then the way of sanctification by faith in Jesus will be made plain in the evening of their earthly course, as in the case of Payson and Duncan, for if it is so with the leaders of God's host, will it not be also with the rank and file?

But O how much better it had been! How much better would it be in the morning of life! How much it would save! How much it would bless the world if it should be twenty years earlier!

Chapter Two - Times and Seasons

Timeliness marks all the works and ways of God. Truth has its seasons and the kingdom of God has its periods.

The kingdom of heaven, says our Saviour, is as a grain of mustard seed, the least of all seeds, but when it is grown it is one of the greatest of plants, tree-like, in which the birds of the air may rest themselves and build nests for their young.

At the right time the seed of the kingdom is ripened and dropped into the earth, along the banks of the river of the waters of Life. And the sown-seed knows the spring-time, and snuffs the sunshine and showers: bursting its prison shell, it sends down its roots for moisture and strength, and sends up its stem for light and air; and comes out in spring freshness and beauty. It has also its summer time when it ripens is fruits, and its autumn for filling the garners.

This is true of every child of God — of every church of Christ upon earth, and of the whole church militant collectively taken. Revivals may have been a novelty in the days of Enos, when men first began socially to call on the name of the Lord; but from that day to this they have been the law of the Kingdom. Times of refreshing from the presence of the Lord may have taken Abel by surprise, at that first altar of God at the east gate of Eden, as they evidently did take Cain by surprise, making him gnash his teeth upon Abel as the murderer, of all martyrs have done. But they were understood to be the order of God's economy in the days of the apostles, and indeed in every age of the world.

Great periods have been marked by great revivals, and great revivals have been characterized by the developments, each one of some one great truth made prominent and powerful, in its application to the experience and life of the church.

The great truths which now have their unchangeable position in the faith and formulas of the church, have been born into the world one by one, and one by one have taken their positions in orderly array in the great family of truths. Like children they have come crying into the world, and like warriors in battle, each has had its own way to fight. Like Damascus blades, each has been tried and tempered in the fire and under the hammer of controversy, and like the martyr throng above, they have all come up to their permanent place in the bright galaxy of truth through much tribulation, with their robes made white in the blood of the slain.

The great foundation truth — the unity of God the alpha of all theological science and of all saving knowledge, had its battle of ages with polytheistic idolatry; but has finally driven its enemy into the dark corners of the world, and if appearances may be trusted, will soon drive it out of the world altogether. And the great top-stone of truth, the head of the corner, the trinity of God, is yet in its conflict, and is yet to be more clearly understood — though already it has battled its way to its place in the faith and holds it in triumph against the assaults of every enemy, while shoutings of Grace! Grace! unto it go up from all true believers.

It would be a work to enlarge the largest heart, and expand the most liberal mind, if it were done as it deserves, to sketch truthfully and graphically the biography of each one of the great evangelical truths comprising the faith. Each one has a life and times of its own, and in comparison the lives and times of men — even the greatest of men —would dwindle into insignificance. Indeed the historical prominence of the great men of the church from Abel and Enoch down to Whitefield and Wesley and Edwards, comes from the fact of their being each one the representative — the embodiment — the incarnation, of some one great truth of revealed religion, in some stage of its development, just as Newton and Copernicus were the representatives of astronomical principles.

Revelation had its stages — two great ones — the old and the new, with many minor ones marking them both; though in the new the various stages were crowded into the time of a single generation, whilst in the old many generations sometimes intervened.

Then when revelation was completed, and given complete to the world, no more to be added, nor anything subtracted, upon pain of God's curse, even then, since that, the development and application of the several truths revealed, has been also by stages. Each in its own time and each in its own way.

The question may have arisen already — and if not there is no reason to shrink from raising it now — why — if it is true that the experimental apprehension of the principle of sanctification by faith is the privilege of all — why has the fact not had greater prominence in the past? Why have eighteen centuries been allowed to roll away before it is brought distinctly and prominently before the mind of the church?

The answer is, that until now the time has never come for it. Now is the time. That it is no new thing, practically, is clear. Abel doubtless understood it practically, at least, and was made strong for martyrdom by it. Enoch lived in it, and was translated, taken bodily to heaven without death by it. Noah built his ark, in the faith of it, and out-rode the flood by it; and Abraham in the power of it forsook the home of his birth and dwelt amongst strangers, and waited patiently for the fulfilment of God's promise — and then himself, at the command of God, was in act to put the knife to the throat of Isaac, the son of promise, counting God able to raise him again from the dead. Prophets, and apostles, and reformers, and the great and good of every age have exemplified it. It is nothing new. And yet, until now, the time has never fully come to give it the prominence which now it is destined to take and to hold in the future history and progress of the Kingdom of God in the world.

It is now only three hundred years since the Bible itself was exhumed from its burial places in convent cells and library alcoves, and freed from its cerements of the dead languages, torn from it by the hand of the reformers, and put in its dress of living speech, and sent forth upon its great mission to the world.

And it is only one hundred years since the great truth of the new birth, as a distinct experience, the privilege of all, began to receive its full power of application to the heart and life of the church. And yet both were just at the opportune moment.

It is beautiful to mark the times and occasions of truth in its connection with the orderly march of events, as in single file, with solemn tread, they come forward at the command of the Lord.

The translation of Enoch was just at the time when the heavens had become overcast with dark clouds of unbelief, and a window in heaven was needed that man might see it, and not forget that there is a heaven above.

The flood came just when the fear of God had died out, and violence had run riot filling the earth; just in time to let all after generations know that there is a God of justice and judgment ruling over all, who does not shrink from wrapping a world in its own winding-sheet, regardless of its agonizing shrieks of despair, if the cry of its guilt and the call of justice demand it.

The overthrow of Babel and the confusion of tongues, was just at that moment when the pride of man and his desire to cast off fear and restrain ·prayer had concentrated and culminated in the great city and tower, which were to be at once both the glory and the safety, and the bond of union of the whole human race. The plan of the mighty hunter and hero and builder, Nimrod, was laid and almost completed. With every successive course of bricks upon the tower, the pride of the people and their feeling of security rose, and the bond of their union was strengthened, and the fear of God weakened. Dependence upon God had ceased. They were now no more afraid to give loose reins to idolatry, and when at the same time through them, in their humility, God could teach the world through His servants in the court, and their influence upon the king, the worship of Jehovah as the one only true God, just in time for the second greatest battle and victory of the true God over idols.

The coming of Christ is happily marked by the apostle as just then when the fulness of time had come. When the Jewish dispensation was waxing old and ready to pass away, and when the Greek was the written language of the world, and the Roman power the governing power of the world, and when the world was all connected in the one empire of Rome, and all open to the apostles and primitive Christians to go with the gospel to every creature, and when idolatry in all the civilized world was in its dotage, the bye-word and laughing stock of the learned. When, in short, there was an open field for a fair contest, such as there never had been before.

The advent of the Holy Spirit, when Pentecost had fully come, was just when the time for it had fully come, also.

Just when the great work of atonement had been finished, the resurrection accomplished, and the risen Saviour had ascended to the right hand of power. Just when a demonstration of his power as the living and almighty Saviour was needed to revive the drooping disciples and convince a gainsaying world. And just when the disciples themselves needed that very baptism of light and love, and peace and power to inspire them with wisdom and boldness and strength for their great commission of giving the gospel to the world.

The breaking down of the Jewish walls of prejudice by Peter's vision and Paul's commission, together with the conversion first of Cornelius and his friends, and afterwards of the Gentiles at Antioch, and the proceedings of the apostles and elders in consequence, was just in time to open the way and set the gospel free to fly abroad, run and conquer, and win the day.

The Reformation, passing by the events of fourteen hundred years — each as timely as any before or after — the Reformation came again just when all things were ready. The corruptions of Rome had gone so far that all good men everywhere longed for reform. And the darkness had become so great as to be felt, and felt, too, in all its oppressive power, so as to create a deep and earnest desire for the light of God's word. The church was in the condition of one in a cavern, or in the catacombs, in whose hand the light has gradually sunk, until at last it has flickered and flared, and expired. When, then, he has wandered on, blundering and stumbling in the dark, until at last he has become afraid to take another step without a light. Just as such an one would hail the light with unspeakable joy, just so the people of that day were prepared to hail the light of the Bible. O, what joy it gave them, when it came forth; now no longer speaking in an unknown tongue, but in every man's own language, wherein he was born. Germans and Brittons; Hollanders and French; Italians and Spaniards; Hungarians and Bavarians; Normans, Danes, Swedes, and all.

Then, too, it should not be forgotten that this was just at the time when the newly discovered art of printing had prepared the way to give wings to the word of God, like the angel of the Apocalypse flying, mid-heaven for its mission, to the nations of the world, as never could have been done before.

The Great Awakening, two hundred years later, now one hundred years ago, was just in time to arrest the lapsing church in its downward course, and give it a great impulse upward and onward in preparation for what has come since, and what is now coming, and what is yet to come in the future. To the great central doctrine of justification by faith revived before in the Reformation, the fact of the new birth, as an experience for all, was now added to the faith of the church in the great awakening. And this just at the moment when the churches of America were in the plastic state, ready to take the Whitefieldian and Wesleyan and Edwardean type, as older churches in older lands were slow to do. And at the moment, too, when India fell under British rule, to be opened to Christianity in due time.

And now in the intervening hundred years, O how great events have thickened. The old slow march seems to have hastened into double quick time, and the single file to have formed up into the order of platoons. The Missionary Era, commencing fifty years ago, just when simultaneously Bibles began to multiply through the multiplying power of Bible societies, and missionaries began to rise up, to go out into all the world, and the church began to combine to send them, and the nations began to throw open their doors to receive them, and commerce began to spread its wings anew to take them, and steam power began to develop the superiority of Christian nations in all the arts of life, and stimulate commerce to carry Christian fabrics into all heathen nations. Just then a new life began in the church, wider the unfolding power of the great commission, which for ages had been allowed to sleep, but now was proclaimed from every pulpit and by every Christian press of Christendom.

As years roll on the natural sciences unfold and lead even skeptical minds to abandon atheism and pantheism and come upon the platform of revelation. All machinery is improved. Railroads are invented. Ships are enlarged, and steam is harnessed in to be our servant of all works on sea and land. Electricity is drilled also into service, and a network of veins and arteries is created, producing a grand system of thought circulation, fast binding the nations together into one, or at least bringing them face to face within speaking distance of each other. The printing press is increased by a thousand-fold in its productive power, and the gold fields of California, Australia, and the north open up their treasures, and pour a golden current into the commercial arteries of the world. And just now, in the midst of all this, God comes down in the power of His spirit and arouses the young men and the business men, the laymen and the laywomen, as well as office bearers in the church, to meet and pray and work for the Master, and such a revival begins as the world has never witnessed before. Hope rises up and begins to stretch forward to the great battle and final triumph. And what now is needed? What now would be the timely work? and what now the timely truth? There is now more than ever needed two things. First, the millenial type of Christian character and life.

Second, the spiritual strength and endurance to carry the church onward and upward unswervingly to and through the conflict and triumph before us. And these two are one, and this one is the experience of full salvation through full trust in the Lord Jesus Christ.

Chapter Three - The Present and the Future

The present is ever the stepping-stone of the future. Each stage of progress is the bud of the next. Conviction prepares the way for conversion; conversion leads to sanctification; sanctification culminates in glory; and glory begun is the entrance upon an endless career of progress in wisdom and knowledge, beneficence and bliss.

In the history of the kingdom, the dread of wrath and death induced by the flood, prepared the way for the law; the law was the school-master to drill the world into readiness for the gospel; the coming of Christ and his death laid the foundations for the temple to be reared by the Holy Spirit, and he is now erecting the temple, stone by stone, course upon course, story above story, in preparation for the millennium and the kingdom of glory.

The present — the now present, would seem to be around in the heavenward-stretching ladder near to the top. One step more, or two at most, so it seems at least to us poor short-sighted mortals and the summit will be gained.

What, then, are the now unfolding germs preparing the way for the incoming period?

Three things may be confidently predicted of the church of the future — its UNITY, ACTIVITY and SPIRITUALITY.

In the prayer of Jesus with his disciples on the night of his betrayal, the unity of his followers was coupled with the spread of the knowledge that Jesus is the Messiah of God as its cause, "That they all may be one," prayed the Saviour, "that the world may know that thou hast sent me."

One! Yes; the disciples of Christ are yet in the future, sometime, sooner or later, to become completely united, and then the world will know that he is the Messiah of God.

This prayer of Jesus is to have its happy fulfilment — When? When, if not in the period next approaching, and now at the doors?

What is the watchword of the present? Union. Fifty years ago now, it may be more or less, God began the visible preparations for the fulfilment of this prayer. First in England. The missionary spirit was poured into the heart of an obscure cobler upon his bench, and as he cut the leather into shape, and pounded it upon his lapstone into solidity, and drew the waxed ends stitching together shoes for his customers, he was cutting out, compacting, and stitching together thoughts, which were destined to shoe the feet of thousands upon thousands with the preparation of the gospel of peace to go to the outer bounds of the earth with the glad tidings of a crucified Saviour.

His discourse delivered — the question was raised. Who will go? and whom shall we send?" His feet were all shod ready for the journey and his ready answer was, "Send a better man if you can – if not, here I am, send me."

This settled — next came the question, How? And the practical answer was, combine, associate. So they combined; a little nucleus, enough to send out and sustain their man.

And this was the first of the many nuclei in that land and in others around which Christians have rallied until now what do we behold? Scores, it may be, of huge corporations, gathering money by millions, and sending out and sustaining missionaries by thousands upon thousands, at home and abroad, amongst the people of every kindred and tongue almost in the world!

The missionary fathers combined, like the early settlers in a new country, in their house "raisings" and "bees," upon the principle that ten men can lift a log into place in the cabin's side which one could not stir from the ground — and
upon the maxim that "many hands make light work."

The movers in the World's Protestant Alliance had other, and in some respects, higher motives for union. They desired to bring the ends of Protestantism together, and in some sort cement all into one, insomuch, at least, as to be able to present to themselves and to their enemies, and to the world, the imposing spectacle of a single front, and the invincible strength of an undivided line of battle.

But it is only now that the highest and noblest movements have begun, in fulfilment of the prayer for unity. Young Christianity is moved to lay aside the grey prejudices of sect, and throw off the dead weight of formality. Associations are formed for the purpose of counteracting the increasing corruptions of our cities in their influence, especially upon the young men drawn from the country, into these great centres of activity and attraction. God pours out his spirit upon these associations, and united young Christianity becomes suddenly converted into a society, not simply to make a fair show before the world of the unity of the church of Christ, nor yet to send into all the world to preach the gospel, but actually to go — every man becoming himself a missionary. Union meetings are started in places and numerical attendance to startle the world, and increased in numbers to reach the masses in every locality. Circles are broken in upon by the evangelizing influence, which have ever been regarded as close corporations in the interest and under the sole control of Satan himself, and voices are heard in praise and prayer which have been wont to make the night and the Sabbath hideous with their yells in the street. And holy hands are lifted to God, and raised also for hearty blows in the cause of the Prince of Peace, raised before never in this way, but often in theatres, in brawls and fights, and in pugilistic contests.

The missionary fathers combined to send a few thousands to set up the standard of the cross, and begin the war in every land. The Alliance movers combined to show and to feel the full strength of the embattled host, not at all for actual contest, but in a sort of world's review from year to year. But now the embattled host is combining, for the contest and the conquest.

Like the "Old Thirteen," in the days of American colonial dependence, the churches have all along known and felt their unity, (in the one Lord, and the one faith, and one baptism, of Christ,) and have often combined for some special practical purpose, or for some sort of colonial congress to declare unity in words and present the show of united resistance to our enemies — but it is only now that every man is harnessing for the war, and taking his position, side by side with every other man, irrespective of denominational distinctions.

And although we are far yet from the fulfilment of the Saviour's prayer, still we were never before so near, never before surrounded by so many tokens and preparations for its fulfilment as now. The unfolding bud is plainly the bud of complete unity — it cannot be mistaken. This unity is to be a unity in Christ, and so it will manifest Christ. The disciples are to see face to face, because they will all see the face of God in Christ and become like him, and so become like each other. Changed from glory to glory into his image, and so changed also from degree to degree into likeness, and love too, to each other, and so showing forth the image of Christ which they have taken.

There is a unity in Christianity which has never been realised in the church, though typified by the nucleus of early converts in the dawn, when bathed and baptized in the first rising beams of the Sun of Righteousness ascended, "they were of one heart, and one soul: neither said any that aught of the things he possessed was his own; but they had all things common." "Then they continued daily with one accord in the temple, and breaking bread from house to house, did eat their meat with gladness and singleness of heart, praising God and having favor with all the people, and the Lord added unto them daily such as should be saved." (Acts iv: 32, and ii. 46, 47)

There has been, and is yet, great discordance in the varied songs of the many churches — but there is to be a universal harmony — nay a universal unity in the one song of Moses and the Lamb, each church bearing its own part in the general concert, and then all earth and heaven shall hear.

Each tone on the musical scale is composed of three — three in one — one in three. And it may be there is one tone — known or unknown — itself three in one, which is the union of all — the grand focal starting point and centre of all.

The primitive rays of the sun are white, but each ray is in itself a combination of three — three in one, one in three. And this one ray — white as it touches first the sphere of earth's vestment of air, is separated by the vapory prism into every hue and shade, clothing the globe in its beauteous coat of clouds of many colors, and carpeting it with green and gold, pink and purple, and every other lovely color and tint, in every form of grace and sweetness. God is light. The rays of the Sun of Righteousness are light, light ineffable, light alone. But they bring embosomed in themselves to him who receives Jesus, the Triune God. And they work out as they fall upon human hearts and human minds, all the separated shades and varied combinations, of grace and truth — one and yet many.

On the face of the cloud in the retiring storm the bow springs forth — the bow of promise — seven beauteous colors are numbered in the exquisite arch. The seven make one arch. And the whole seven spring from one — the one white ray of the sun separated into seven, and bent together into the symbol of harmony and of hope.

Christ is the one. The churches are the seven. And the one in the seven, is Christ in the heart the hope of glory.

Already the bow of harmony and of hope, as we have seen, is springing forth, upon the face of the retiring darkness and strife of the past. The day of unity is at hand.

Activity is equally, also, both the demand of the future and the promise unfolding in the present to meet this demand.

The church of the future is to be a living church. Every member a living member — every one doing his duty.

Too much, in all the past, since the first and glorious days of the apostles, went by; the church has been a sort of hospital or asylum, where its members have been gathered in to be cared for and nursed — provided for and dosed, or taught, like the infirm, the deaf and dumb and the blind; and ministers and officers of the church have been engrossed in their cares of the various inmates of the churches.

But now it is to be hoped the church is becoming more like a force of able-bodied industrials, ready for employment in the Master's vineyard, under the guidance of ministers and officers. Helpers together with God, not cumberers of his ground. Certainly there never has been a time, since the apostolic age, when the opportunities were so general or so generally accepted and used by all Christians, especially the young, to engage in the active spread of the gospel amongst the perishing myriads around. And there never was a time when so many had the boldness to "stand up for

Jesus" as witnesses before great assemblies, or go out for Jesus into the hard places, and to the hard cases of the world. Activity — increasing activity — growing steadily toward universality, is certainly one of the unfolding promises of the present.

Spirituality, also. If we look to see its increase in the increase of the three abiding graces — faith, hope and charity — and of the four cardinal virtues — prayers, gifts, words and works for Jesus — more beautiful in their blended symmetry than the seven colors of the bow in the cloud, we shall not fail of a certain promise and prophecy of a bright day at hand. When has there ever been so much, or so fervent, or so simple praying, or so great faith of the answers to prayer, or so much life and power in the religious meetings, or so much wayside conversation about the works and ways of God?

Not now, however, to dwell upon this. Looking rather to the bow of promise, arching the heavens, as the gateway of the future. What are the three words traced by the finger of Providence along the front of this royal arch? What but the triune promise, unity, activity and spirituality?

And now to ask and answer again more at large the question asked and answered in the conclusion of the preceding chapter. What do we now need to swell and unfold this triune promise into the universality and strength required for its own happy fulfilment?

Simply the prevalence of a full experimental union with Jesus by a full trust in his name.

Our union of the future is not to be one merely of convenience or interest, or necessity, to accomplish the work given us to do; but the union of heart and soul, vital as the union of the several members of one's own body. And our activity is not to be that of excitements and occasions, or of the pressure of duty merely, but the increased activity which comes from increased vitality. Life within — life more abundant — must be the sustaining power and central spring of the increased life without. And our spirituality will be made full by the full indwelling presence and power of the Spirit of God.

We need, therefore, to turn attention increasingly to the higher form of Christian experience. Not by any means to lose sight of conversion, but rather to press it more urgently than ever upon the attention of the world; but not as the all in all — not as the stopping place of the Christian, or as introducing the convert into all the fulness of the blessings of the gospel of peace.

Suppose Luther had been content to rest where he was when he first found the forgiveness of his sins in the convent at Erfurth, and had not pressed on until he found also the way of full justification, including sanctification from sin. What would have been the result?

Simply that he might have remained a monk, after all, to the end of his days, and the Reformation untouched by him to the last. It was the final, full conscience of the way of salvation by faith, into which the Lord introduced him on Pilate's staircase at Rome, and not his conversion at Erfurth, merely, that made him the reformer he was. And D'Aubigne. Suppose he, too, had never passed beyond the first great stage of his experience, but remained to the end where he was during the years after his conversion at Geneva, and before his second conversion at the inn-room in Kiel; where now had been his great work, the History of the Reformation, and other like works, bearing the stamp of his faith as well as the stamp of his genius? Unwritten, unwritten; every word of them unwritten.

Two books, (Narratives of Remarkable Conversions, Conant. Derby & Jackson, N. Y. The Divine Life, Kennedy. Parry & McMillen, Philadelphia; Presbyterian Board) of very great value and of deservedly wide circulation — may their circulation be a hundred fold greater — have been recently given to the public. In both, the experience of Luther is professedly given, and truly as far as they go. And in one, also, that of D'Aubigne. But in each instance the narrative stops short with conversion, leaving in each the after and deeper experience untold, without so much as an allusion, even. The after and deeper experience, without which neither the one or the other would have been qualified by the faith of Jesus in its fulness, or the light of the gospel in its power, for the work and the mission so happily and so nobly fulfilled by them.

The same thing is true, also, of Baxter and Hewitson and others whose conversions are narrated in the two volumes referred to, but Luther and D'Aubigne are singled out because both of their exalted position in the regards of the church, of every name in every land, and also, and especially, of the ample distinctness of their own narrations of their own experiences, in the second great stage as well as the first; and because also of the illustration, peculiarly impressive, in their cases, that the second experience is the indispensable requisite of power to glorify God in the highest degree, by witnessing for Jesus in the fullest, freest, boldest, clearest manner.

This omission is very significant. One of the straws showing the drift of the popular current. It indicates a great historical fact and phase of the present, and a glorious one it is — only less glorious than the more excellent phase of the future. It shows the profound absorption of the mind and heart of the church in the matter of conversion.

But then does it not also show the almost equally profound forgetfulness of the deeper experience exemplified by these great and good men, their second conversion?

This ought not so to be — must not be so.

The keynote of pulpit and press now for a hundred years, and the clarion note as well — sounding out so loud and clear as to rule every other into the harmonious line with itself on the theological staff — has been the new birth. May it never lose one particle of its clarion clearness. Rather let it be sounded out a thousand fold louder and clearer than ever until it shall reach every ear, and every heart in the world, thrilling them with its heavenly power.

But then, in the baptism of John, are we to forget the baptism of Jesus? In the new birth shall we forget the deeper power of Pentecost? In the regeneration by water and the Spirit shall we lose sight of the deeper regeneration by fire and the Spirit?

The new birth is indeed a reality and a blessed one, an experience and an indispensable one, and may it be urged in all the burning, convincing power of the spirit of Elias. So also is the baptism of the Holy Ghost a reality and a more glorious one. Let it be also urged in the spirit and power of the apostles.

The disciples of Jesus needed and received the promise of the Father upon them, conferring the power to be effectual witnesses for Jesus in the introduction of the gospel in its fulness into the world? Do we not need, shall we not receive the same blessed promise in all the fulness of its plenary power — the miraculous only excepted — for the struggle of its final victory and the introduction of its glorious fulfilment in the world?

But a case so plain is only weakened by arguments, as if arguments were needed to establish it, when, in fact, it is self-evident at a glance.

One illustration of the power and blessedness of full salvation may suffice to close this chapter, and this part of our discussion.

A better might be looked for in vain than the following parable from life, of...

The Judge and the Poor African

In one of the populous and beautiful towns on the banks of "La Belle Riviere," the Ohio, there dwelt and for aught I know, dwells now a just judge, honorable in life as well as in title; and also a poor lone African woman, long since gone to her crown and her throne in the kingdom above. She was queenly in the power and beauty of her spiritual progress, though poor as poverty could make her in this world's goods here upon earth, but she is now doubtless queenly in position and external adorning as well as in heart, transformed and transfigured in the presence of the glorious Saviour in heaven, whom she loved so dearly and trusted so fully upon earth.

The judge was rich and highly esteemed. He dwelt in a mansion, not so fine as to repel, not so splendid as to make him the envy of the foolish, large enough to be the social centre of the town, and plain enough to make every one feel it a home, and his heart was in keeping with his house, large and open.

The poor African woman lived in a cabin on an alley all alone without chick or child, kith or kin.

Her own hands ministered amply to her own wants while she had health, and at home or abroad at work by the day, she often earned that which found its way to India, or Africa perhaps, in the spread of the gospel. Her home though poor and small was always neat and tidy. She belonged to the church of which the judge was an officer, and often sat down with him at the table of the Lord, in the house of the Lord, as she will again, O how joyously at the feast of the Bridegroom in the palace of the King, but it so happened that they had never had free conversation together about the things of the kingdom. He respected her. She venerated him. At last she received a severe injury, from which she never recovered, and for many weary months before her death was dependent and helpless, alone and bed-rid.

During this time the judge's ample table and abundant wardrobe had contributed its full share to the comforts of the poor woman. Never a day but she was remembered. But for a long time, for one reason and another, he put off from time to time a personal visit which yet he fully purposed in his heart to make her. Until at last one day as he thought of the cheeriness of his own pleasant home the thought of the contrast between this and the loneliness and desolation of the poor woman's cabin came into his mind, and while it heightened his gratitude for the goodness of God to him, it filled him with sadness and sympathy for her.

"Who can tell but I may cheer her a little, and perhaps by a little timely sympathy save her from repining at her hard lot? Possibly, too, I may be able to throw some light upon the rugged pathway along which she is going to the
  kingdom?"

The judge loved to do good; it was a great luxury to him. So, taking a well-filled basket, and making sure that purse as well as scrip was stored with convenient small change, he sallied forth to visit the poor woman.

As the door opened, he was struck with the air of neatness in the cabin. If she was bed-rid, some kind hand supplied the place of her's. Everything was in order, swept and garnished neat as a pin. "Not so desolate after all," thought he.

But again, as the judge looked around, and contrasted the social joys of his own ample mansion, where the voice of children and of music, as well as the presence of books and friends made all cheerful and happy, with the cheerless solitude of the poor woman alone here from morning till night and from night till morning, only as one or another called out of kindness to keep her from suffering, his heart filled again with sadness and sympathy.

Seating himself on the stool at the side of the poor woman's cot, he began speaking to her in words of condolence:

"It must be hard for you, Nancy, to be shut up here alone so many days and weeks?"

"O no, thank God, massa judge, the Good Lord keeps me from feelin bad. I'se happy now as ever I was in all my days."

"But, Nancy, laying here from morning till night and from night till morning all alone, and racked with pain, dependent upon others for everything, do you not get tired and down-hearted, and think your lot a hard one to bear?"

"Well, I'se 'pendent on others, dat's sure, 'deed I is, an I was allers used to have something to give to de poor, an to de missionary, too, an to de minister, but den I'se no poorer dan my good Lord was when he was here in de worl, and I'se nebber suffer half so much yet as he suffer for me on de cross. I'se bery happy when I tink of dese tings."

"But, Nancy, you are all alone here?"

"Yes, massa, I'se all alone, dat's true, but den Jesus is here, too, all de time. I'm nebber alone, no how, and he's good company."

"But, Nancy, how do you feel when you think about death? What if you should die here all alone some night?"

"O, massa judge! I spect to. I spect nothing else but jes to go off all alone here some night, as you say, or some day. But it's all one, night or day, to poor Nancy, and den, massa, I spec I'll not go all alone after all, for Jesus says, in de blessed Book, I'll come an take you to myself dat where I am dare you may be also, an I believe him. I'se not afraid to die alone."

"But, Nancy, sometimes when I think of dying, I am filled with trouble. I think how bad I am, what a sinner, and how unfit for heaven, and I think now what if I should die suddenly just as I am, what would become of me? Are you not afraid to die and go into the presence of a holy God?"

"O no, massa 'deed I'se not."

"Why not, Nancy?"

"O, massa, I was 'fraid, berry much. When I was fust injer, I see I mus die, an I thought how can such a sinner as I is ebber go into such a holy place as de new Jerusalem is? An I was miseble, O, I was miseble, deed, sure! But den by an by, after a while, I jis thought I mus trus myself to do blessed Jesus to make me ready for de kingdom jis as I did to forgib all my sins. An so I foun res for my poor soul in Jesus, an sen dat time I feel some-how, all better; I know now he will make me all ready pure an white for de new Jerusalem above. An now I love to think about de time when I shall come to 'pear befo the Father's throne, wid him in glory, all starry spangly white."

For a moment the judge sat in silence, admiring the power of grace. Not yet himself deeply affected by the light reflected from this star in disguise. A little pressure more was required — another chafing question — to bring out the ray destined to pierce his own soul.

"Well, Nancy, one thing more let me ask you; Do you never complain?"

"Complain! O, now massa judge, complain, do you say, massa? Why, massa! Who should such a one as I is complain ob! The Good Lord He knows bes what's bes for poor Nancy! His will be done!"

Nancy said this in tones of the deepest sincerity. And a little more. There was just a shade of wonder at the question — as much as to say, "What: you an officer in the church, and a man of education, a judge, and yet think that a poor creature like me might complain of the dealings of a merciful God and Saviour like mine?"

The arrow took effect. The judge bowed his head in silence a moment, and then rose and bade Nancy good-bye, without the word of consolation and prayer, which he fully purposed when he went into the cabin.

All the way home he kept saying to himself, "Well, I never yet said 'His will be done' in that way. I never felt it. Alone, poor, helpless, bedrid, dependent, miserable in body, and yet happy as an angel. Ah! there is a power there I never felt. But I must feel it, and God helping me I will. Not afraid to die. Trusting Jesus to purify her from all sin, and present her spotless before God. Waiting joyously his summons. O, blessed faith! I must know more of this, and I will."

Two weeks, night and day, the arrow rankled, rankled, rankled. His pain increased. Sleep forsook him, and his family became alarmed. He said nothing, but often groaned in spirit and sighed deeply. Sometimes the tears were seen to steal down his manly cheeks. All wondered, and all waited to hear what had come over the strong mind and manly heart of the judge.

At last, one day while he was bowed before God, he felt in his heart "Thy will be done." The storm-tossed sea of his soul was suddenly calmed, and peace filled his heart — peace as a river. Now he, too, could trust Jesus to make for him his pathway on earth and fit him for heaven, and take him to it whenever amid from whatever place it might please him.

It was the beginning of a new life for him — a change quite as great as at the time of his conversion, and as it has proved, the beginning of blessed things for his own family and church and town, and for the cause of Christ generally. Consistent and steadfast before, he has been a burning and a shining light, letting his light shine far and near ever since.

He went in the fulness of wealth and education, and influence and honor, to the poor, lone, lorn African woman, to do her good if he might with either counsel or food, or clothing or money. This was the full purpose and prayer of his heart; and yet, while he gave nothing to her, he received from her what all his wealth could not purchase or all his wisdom devise.

She, poor body, had nothing to give, nor so much as even dreamed of giving aught to anybody. And yet, without a thought of it, she did give to the rich and honorable judge what was worth more to him than the wealth and honors of all the world.

And what does this illustrate to us? What but the power of spirituality? What but the power which poured upon the few illiterate fishermen of Galilee in the Pentecostal baptism, fitted them for the reformation of the world, almost in a single generation? What but the very power now needed to transform the world and introduce the golden age of complete gospel triumph?

Chapter Four - The Christian Life

ITS ABIDING GRACES AND ABIDING FORCES.

Too many learn how to live just when they come to die. The great principles which give men peace in the hour of death, would have given them power, had they known them throughout their lives. These great principles have been the property of the few in the past, as the joy of their pathway and the power of their usefulness in life, while the many ten thousands of Israel have waited until driven into them by the stern necessities of the dying hour, and then with Dr. Payson and Gov. Duncan, they have poured into the ears of God and man, the singularly commingled notes of extatic delight in their newly made discoveries of the wonders of God's wisdom and grace in the plan of salvation — and of regret that these discoveries had not been made by them with the rising instead of the setting sun of their Christian course in the world.

The experience in question — in the main — is the whole-hearted reception

of the true principles of the Christian life in their full-orbed proportions. Learning to live, not simply learning to die.

Mainly we have been content to present these, the true principles, in contrast with the false, in the vain struggles of struggling ones in their futile attempts to find peace and purity by the wrong course, and in the triumphant issue in every case the moment the right course was entered upon. It is due yet more fully to present the true and the false in contrast in their subsequent manifold workings in all the practical progress of the subsequent life, and in all the questions of duty and difficulty by which the disciple of Jesus may be perplexed in his course.

A field for a volume in itself, which however must be compressed to a space bounded by the lines and landmarks of a few chapters at most.

According to St. Paul, the abiding graces of the Christian life, are Faith, Hope and Charity; these are also its abiding forces, at once gracious, grateful and powerful. Gracious as the merciful gifts of God's ineffable love, and graceful as chief ornaments of the disciples of Jesus — the royal regalia of kings and priests unto God — the clothing of wrought gold all beautiful within of the bride, the Lamb's wife — they are also the great permanent forces wrought and employed by the Spirit of God for the development and progress of the Divine Life in the soul, and for its outraying influence, giving light to a world sitting in darkness and in the shadow of death. All the progress vouchsafed to the disciple of Jesus, whether in the transformation of his own character into the image of his Master, or in aiding others to become with him partakers of the divine nature, is traceable directly to these three graces and forces of the life of God in the soul.

The germinal start of Christianity in the world, was given it, it is true, by these three permanent forces — not alone — but aided by three others, occasional in their nature — inspiration, miracles and persecutions. These three occasional forces, each in its own measure and way, but all with the hand of the mighty, came in as helpers in producing the three permanent forces, faith, hope and charity, tending directly, like the protecting glass of the green house in aid of the sun to give a vigorous and early expansion to that which otherwise had been of much slower growth.

Inspiration caused the unmingled and undimmed light of the Sun of Righteousness to shine forth in the apostolic teachings vouchsafed to the primitive church. The simplicity and directness with which the apostles, like the herald of Christ on the banks of the Jordan, pointed to Jesus as the Lamb of God which taketh away — beareth away — purgeth away the sins of the world, is wonderful. And wonderfully contrasted too with subsequent instructions, miracles, like inspiration, pointed also directly to Jesus, in aid of faith in his name.

No miracle ever wrought by the hand of an apostle, was ever wrought save in the name of Jesus. And even to the face of their fierce persecutors, before whom to confess Jesus, was a crime punishable with death, the apostles gave always and only the name of Jesus, as him who through faith in his name made the cripple to leap for joy, the blind to see and the diseased to stand up in their presence made whole. Every miracle was therefore a demonstration that all power on earth and in heaven was centered in Jesus, and every miracle proclaimed therefore the name of Jesus as the only name given under heaven amongst men whereby we must be saved. And moreover every miracle was in itself a practical ocular proof, that Christ was then and there present in power — though absent and invisible in body — a very present help, mighty and able to deliver, able to do exceeding abundantly above all they could ask or think according to the power which they saw at work with their own eyes.

Persecution, also in its own bloody way, tended, though far from its wish, to build up the faith, which in its impotent wrath it sought to destroy. Most effectually persecution crucified the disciple of the crucified Jesus to the world, and the world to him.

With bloody hand it pointed to Jesus, and bade the disciple choose between him and the world — Jesus, with imprisonment, torture and death — or the world, with life, liberty and peace — was the alternative persecution proposed. And he who chose the Redeemer, could be no half-hearted one, either in his faith, or his hope, or his love, centered in Christ.

Martyrdom made martyr spirits of thousands who were not themselves called to the stake or the cross. And the martyr spirit which shines out with such lustre from dungeon cells and fiery faggots, is bright also, and beautiful and powerful, in the bosom of a church unmolested, and in times of profoundest peace.

These, however, were only the conservatory influences, especially used by the Great Hushandman above, for the early and vigorous development of Christianity in the days of its budding existence in the world. The vine in its maturity, transplanted into every chime and soil under the whole heaven was left, as it has now been left nearly eighteen hundred years, to battle with the elements under divine training and culture by virtue of its three great permanent forces, faith, hope and love.

Inspiration passed away when the sacred oracles were filled up and complete.

Miracles, as the seal of divine inspiration, ceased with inspiration itself.

And persecution, always fitful, employed, only as the wrath of man could be made to praise God, was restrained in its remainder, and long since has nearly passed away forever.

Now abide these three, Faith, Hope and Charity. And if the greatest of these three is charity, because by and by faith is to be swallowed up in sight and hope in fruition, leaving charity only as the finally abiding one of the three in heaven. Yet faith in another sense is the greatest here upon earth, as the first in the order of enumeration not only, but also of reception and working.

If love is necessary to faith to make it saving, faith is necessary to love for its very existence.

If faith without love is but a sounding brass and a tinkling cymbal, love without faith would be less yet, nothing at all, it could not be.

The plan of God in its profound wisdom and powerful working is simply this, to charm the sinner into love for God by making him see God's love for the sinner. The fulness of his love God has shown in the gift of his only begotten Son to die for the sins of the world. And faith, while it is the hand of the soul to receive and appropriate the gift as offered from God in his gospel, is also the eye of the soul to perceive the ineffable love which dictated the gift, and it is the sight of this wonderful love of God for the sinner which melts the heart of the sinner into love for God in return.

Faith then, in the absence of vision, and until sight takes its place, is the mainspring of love and so the mainspring of life.

Angels and the just made perfect have no need of faith, because they stand in the presence of Jehovah, Jesus, and behold his glory and are kindled into rapture thereby.

Faith, to us, supplies the place of sight, as far as it can, and as far as we have it, by depicting our God and Saviour to us as revealed in his works and word.

Hope is only another aspect and application of faith.

Faith is the second sight of the soul given of God to enable us to realize invisible things of the present. And hope is this same second sight of the soul turned toward the realities of the future.

The apostle himself in his epistle to the Hebrews, xi. 1, includes both faith and hope in the one definition, while yet in that definition he distinguishes clearly the distinctive aspects and powers of the two.

"Faith," he says, "is the substance of things hoped for, the evidence of things not seen."

Faith in the aspect of hope, pushes forward to the end of the world and beyond into the kingdom of glory, and brings back the olive leaf promise; nay the very substance of all the glories which are outspread in their infinite duration and boundless blessedness, this side and especially beyond the tomb and beyond the judgment, while faith, as the second sight of invisible realities in the present, is the evidence to us, of what Christ has already done for us, in tasting death for our sins, and what he is now to us in his living presence, power, care and love watching over us from day to day, and guiding us in all the struggles and issues of the present here upon earth, and what he is now for us also, as our advocate, mediator and friend in heaven above.

The apostle illustrates this, his two-fold definition of faith by calling up as witnesses, the illustrious cloud of the holy men of old, from Abel onwards, until he himself is swallowed up in the cloud and ceases from sheer inability to enumerate the bright host gone before.

Enoch exemplified both the faith which realizes the presence of God here, and the faith which is the substance of glory hoped for hereafter. Enoch walked with God by faith as the second sight of invisible realities in the present. By faith he saw God and saw what would please him — and gained this testimony that he did please him in the then present time.

By faith as a second sight, a prophetic vision of things in the future, Enoch was not, for God took him. He looked up to, and longed for, and was translated into the kingdom of glory, without having died.

So Enoch's faith was first and efficaciously the evidence of things not seen in the present, and then, and most gloriously, the substance of things hoped for in the future.

Noah, by faith of invisible realities in the present, feared God more than he feared the scoffs and jeers and violence of the bloody generation who filled the world with their deeds of terror, and in spite of all they could do and say built the ark amongst them, animated and sustained by the presence of the invisible God realized to him through faith.

And by faith as a hope of the future he entered the ark and outrode the flood, which swallowed up the whole infidel world, and saw the morn of a new world even this side of death.

Abraham, like Enoch, by faith evidencing to him the invisible realities of the present, walked also with God, abandoning his home, dwelling in tents in a strange land, and offering up Isaac, the son of his love and his hope, counting God able to raise him up from the dead.

And by faith as the substance of things hoped for in the future, Abraham also grasped the mighty future of God's covenant promise, both as it related to his seed after him to be as the stars of heaven innumerable, and also as it related to the city which hath foundations whose builder and maker is God, eternal in the heavens, for himself and his seed.

Moses, by faith as a hope, making the future as real to him as the actual present, and far more glorious, while yet his faith was imperfect and weak, and his character undisciplined, abandoned Pharaoh's court, and refused to be called the son of Pharaoh's daughter, because he had respect unto the recompense of reward, choosing rather to suffer affliction with the people of God than to enjoy the pleasures of sin for a season.

And afterwards — forty years after — when called of God to the work of delivering his people — which forty years before he had presumptuously undertaken, being as yet uncalled — failed not as in the first attempt, because God was now with him as he was not before. And he was sustained by faith as the evidence of invisible realities in the present, mightier than the visible realities opposing him; and so, in the strength of a present God, he was able to endure the wrath of the king, the murmurs of the people, and all the toils and trials incident to breaking the yoke of a tyrannical monarch, and leading out a vacillating, ignorant multitude, and sustaining, training, organizing and disciplining them into the form and order of a compact nation.

In all these, and all the others instanced by the apostle, if time permitted us to cite them, we have illustrations of the two aspects of faith — one as the substance of things hoped for in the future, and the other as the evidence of things unseen in the present.

Faith and hope, then, although different as forces in the development of the Christian life, are yet only one and the same thing in their nature in two different aspects; the one turned toward the invisible realities of the present, and the other toward the certainties of the future; the one resting upon Jesus for what he has already done for us and what he now is for us in heaven, and to us upon earth, and the other resting also upon Jesus for what he is yet to do for us and be to us in time and eternity; the one is the gift of present sight, revealing present things to the blind, else all unseen, and the other is telescopic vision, penetrating far away into the future, and bringing near the glorious things else all hidden from view in the dim distance ahead.

Love, as we have already seen, and seen how, is the offspring of Faith begotten of Grace. By grace are ye saved — saith the apostle — through faith, and that not of yourselves; it is the gift of God.

God's gift is faith. Faith beholds the glorious grace of God in Christ Jesus, and kindles into hope and melts into love.

We see, then, that faith is the all-inclusive gift of God, as the great force for sustaining and developing the Christian life, as we have already before seen that it is the all-inclusive condition of its commencement, verifying the apostle's saying, and the Reformer's experience, that "The just shall live, as well as be made alive by faith." For faith includes hope and produces love.

Before passing to consider the false principles too frequently substituted for the true, as the means of advancing in the divine life, it may be well to have an illustration of the sustaining power of faith.

It happened to the writer to become personally acquainted and associated with one whose life deserves to be sketched by the pen of a Legh Richmond, or a Hannah More, and placed side by side width the Dairyman's Daughter and the Shepherd of Salisbury Plain, in every household of the world.

THE MINER OF POTOSI

We met, first of all, and repeatedly, at the cabin of a woman who opened her doors to a prayer-meeting from week to week on Tuesday evening.

At this proseuchia, (prayer-place) — as yet there was no synagogue (church) in the Hollow, as it was called — the miner had long been wont to meet a fellow-disciple, and sometimes two, or even three, to pour out their hearts before God, and hold up the standard of the cross amidst the surrounding darkness.

It seems that Satan had his seat there, and when the disciples of Jesus came there, he stoutly withstood them as in days of old. It was first called Snake Hollow, from the circumstance of finding a snake in the cavern, where the lead ore was first discovered, and for years the trail of the serpent seemed to be upon everything. The name was afterwards changed to Potosi, and the new name, suggestive of mineral wealth, was not without its significance as to spiritual riches. The pearl of great price was there found by not a few; pearls and diamonds also, were there polished into rare brilliance and beauty for the Master's crown in the day when he shall make up his jewels.

The first Herald of the Gospel who was known to pass through the winding street down the Hollow, was followed by certain lewd fellows of the baser sort — bearing rule there at the time — with empty whiskey barrels. Loose stones were put in at the hung for the noise they would make. They rolled the barrels rapidly on, up to the very heels of the minister's horse, with hootings and howlings, if possible to frighten the horse, and make him run with his rider and throw him. But both horse and rider were too cool for their assailants. They made their way in safety out of the place.

The next minister — fared better — shall I say? Hardly. He sent an appointment before, and in due time following his appointment he went on for its fulfilment. The place selected was a vacant log cabin, and his pulpit the clay hearth at one end of the cabin, under the open hole in the roof, which, when a fire was kindled on the hearth, served as a chimney of escape for the smoke as it rose. There on the hearth the preacher took his stand, while before him a dozen or twenty men were seated on boards across stones, and upon boxes and nail-kegs, butter-firkins and other extempore affairs, common to such places and times.

He had not gone far in his service, however, before strange sounds were heard over his head — a terrible thumping, as of men's hands striking hard upon a table — a sort of table-rapping above; and oaths, the loudest and vilest imaginable, showing the spirits not to be disembodied at least. Looking up, what should be seen there but these same lewd fellows of the whiskey-barrel affair, seated around the hole in the roof, with a board laid across from knee to knee, with their feet dangling below, playing cards. He went on, however, in spite of it, to the end, and the worship of God triumphed over the attempts at disturbance.

An occasional exercise of the Sabbath there was this: In the morning, they gathered in force a hundred, or two hundred, strong, at the head of the Hollow. Organized in mock-Indian-military order, with one of themselves as a chieftain in command. And after copious refreshings of whiskey, they marched in single file — a fiddle solo ahead for their band — with yells a la Indian, making the bluffs reverberate on either side of the Hollow, down the whole length of the winding-way, stopping to refresh and dance, and screech at each of the many drinking-places by the street side. God had better things, however, in store for them. Amongst others — and one of the best — the Lord sent our miner there to pitch tent and delve both for the lead ore in the earth, and for the unfading and unfailing treasures above. One of the early standard-bearers, he, with the consent and to the delight of the good woman at whose house we first met, planted the standard at her house, and gave his colors to the breeze in sight of all in the place. By-and-by, the place filled up, even to overflowing. Then other cabins were open on other evenings of the week. Then a long, log-store was rented and fitted up as a church. Then a church was built. So the prosenchia grew at last into a synagogue, and many will date their conversion to God at that Bethel in the mines.

We met afterward at his own house, or cabin — for cabin it was — one room with a loft, reached by a ladder in one corner. A chest serving the purpose of bureau and sofa, between meals, and settee at the table; a bed in each of the two corners farthest from the hearth, two or three stools, a few pots, skillets, crocks and dishes, and a looking-glass, comprising the furniture. He was tall and manly, graceful and dignified — accustomed to refinement and good society.

He had previously told me that he was reared in old Virginia, in the ease and affluence of heirship to a plantation and servants; and had left there, for conscience sake, with his servants, to provide for them and set them free in a free State. That he had then embarked what had remained to him, in merchandise, in a promiscuous credit-trade in the prairie land of the Northwest, and there had lost almost everything through failure of debtor after debtor to pay him their dues. That he had followed one of the largest of these to the mines, hoping there — by patient waiting in the presence of his debtor, the turn of the wheel, that he might sometime realize the fair promises the debtor was abundant in making. And that there, little by little, all he had left had gone to feed and clothe himself and his family, until now, stripped of all, he was dependent upon the daily earnings of his own naked hands, delving with spade and pick, for ore in the earth for the daily support of his wife and little ones.

But the cheerful tone and happy face of the man as he told the tale of his losses, could not but strike one as wonderful.

Meeting him at his cabin, he welcomed me heartily, gave me a stool, took my hat, and urged me to stay. After the warm greetings were over I asked him how many children he had. Looking fondly upon the three little girls and one little boy gathered at his knees and mine, he answered:

"Five — four here as you see, and," looking up with an expression which seemed to have borrowed both its peace and its joy from heaven above, "one there."

Ah! there spoke out the faith, with its telescope turned heavenward, the very substance of things hoped for!

And then I saw the power which sustained him so joyously in his privations, and toils, and trials, her upon earth.

A cabin could well serve him — as a tent served the patriarchs of old, for his eye was fixed upon a house not made with hands eternal in the heavens.

But this was not all. We met often afterwards and always with pleasure and profit to me. Once in particular, when his words gave me an insight into his faith in its other aspect as the evidence of things present not seen.

A missionary excursion was suggested, requiring a journey of eighty miles in all, and an absence of several days from our homes. The miner was always ready for every good word and work, and his excellent wife, whose faith was as strong and whose heart was as warm, as her husband's, was always ready to consent to his absence when the service of the Master seemed to require it.

Calling at his cabin to consult him, his good wife directed me to his diggings, a mile or so over the hills. There was a little snow on the ground, and I traced his path until I found him. But I should have never known him by his looks. Always before when I had seen him, it was in dress of former days — a little rusty as to fashion, but really rich and genteel, and very becoming to his large and graceful person, but now he was in miner's garb, covered with red clay from the crown of his slouched hat to the sole of his feet — face, hands, clothes and all — a red clay man in appearance. And as I came up to the heap of earth thrown up from the hole where he was digging, and looked down upon the planter-merchant in his miner's disguise, I could not believe it was him, although I looked down full into his upturned face. "Ah, my friend," I exclaimed, "is this you?"

He caught all that was in my heart in the tone of wonder with which the question was asked. But instead of being saddened by the thought of his poverty and toil, he was kindled into joy at the thought of Him who, in his wisdom had permitted it all. And with an expression which made the very clay on his face radiant with the peace of God, he in turn exclaimed, pointing upward,

"'Tis He, appoints our daily lot, and He does all things well."

There spoke out the faith which realizes a very present God in all his wisdom, power and love, working all things together for good to them that love him, the called according to his purpose.

And here again, as in the case of Enoch, and Noah, and Abraham, and Moses, we have the twofold aspect of faith exemplified, the faith of the present and the faith of the future. And in the two we have the combined force appointed of God, to sustain His children in the crucible discipline of life, and bring them forth from the fires, if seven times heated, only by it, seven times purified from the dross of corruption.

Like Paul and Silas, in prison, thrust into the innermost dungeon, fast in the stocks, lacerated with stripes, and covered with blood, yet singing praises to God spite of all, our miner was not only sustained from sinking into despondency and despair, but made more joyous than he had ever been in the sunniest hours of his youth and in the brightest days of his highest prosperity.

Chapter Five - The Contrast

"WHO SHALL DELIVER ME FROM THE BODY OF THIS DEATH? I THANK GOD, THROUGH JESUS CHRIST OUR LORD."

There are Christians of two classes in the world — not to mention others at present — both fond of the apostolic saying placed as a motto above, but very different in experience and position.

They of the one class repeat only the first part of the text — the question — leaving off the answer to it. That gives the key to their experience. They of the other class repeat both question and answer, with intelligent zest. Those of the first class have come to the full and painful understanding of sin dwelling in them as a body of death. Chained to them as a Roman soldier was chained for years to the Apostle Paul; and as dead bodies have been chained to living men. They have come to feel the bondage of sin, but they have not yet come to know the joys of deliverance, and the sweet liberty of the children of God.

Not that they are not Christians. Not that they have never been converted to God. They have been truly converted, or the name Christian, would be a misnomer for them. But they have learned only that their sins are forgiven through faith in the atonement of Jesus. They have not yet learned that Jesus through faith in his name is the deliverer from the power of sin, as well as from its penalty. They believe in the blood of Jesus as their sacrifice for sin, but they are struggling by resolution, with Jesus to aid it — it may be — to free them from the bondage of sin.

Perhaps they have come along so far as to see and feel that resolution, even in the strength of Christ, is a poor deliverer, that it fails ever and anon. And yet they see nothing better, and so they cry out, Who shall deliver me from the body of this death?

And there they stop. There their experience stops. So far they have come, but no farther. While they, of the second class referred to, ask the question, indeed, Who shall deliver me from the body of this death? but answer it in the same breath by finishing the quotation, in the apostle's exulting words: I thank God, through Jesus Christ our Lord.

They have learned that there is deliverance now here in this life through faith in Jesus. While the others sigh and groan in their bondage as if there was no deliverance this side the grave. They have learned experimentally, they know, that Jesus Christ our Lord, through faith in his name, does actually deliver the trusting soul from the cruel bondage of its chains under sin, now in this present time; while the others have learned — not that Jesus does deliver — but that their own resolutions in Jesus' name, do not deliver them; and not knowing that Jesus can do it, they turn with a sigh toward death as their deliverer from the power of this death, as if death was the sanctifier or the sanctification of the children of God.

They of the one class, if asked for the truest and most graphic delineation of the Christian's condition in life here in this world of temptation and sin, will point to the seventh chapter of Romans, and say, "There you have it. That, of all others, describes our state and our struggles here below — a law in our members warring with the law in our minds. We see the right but do the wrong. We would do good but evil is present with us. We resolve, but soon, alas, sin overcomes us. Then we resolve, no more in our own strength, but now in the strength of the Lord. And yet, notwithstanding this fortifying of resolution by acknowledging its weakness and looking to Christ for aid to keep it from breaking — alas, it is soon broken, all the same as before."

They of the other class, if asked for the inspired symbol of their condition, would point us to the eighth chapter of Romans, and say: "There you have it. Once, indeed, we were in the seventh, but thanks be to God, through our Lord Jesus Christ, who has given us deliverance from the body of death, we have now found our way out of the bondage of the seventh, into the sweet liberty of the eight. The chain is broken by the power of Christ. We are freed from the dead body of sin. We are now linked by the three-fold cords of faith, hope and love, to the living Saviour as our deliverer from present corruption, and from all the power of sin.

The dead body is dropped. The living Jesus, sweet Jesus, precious Jesus, gracious Saviour, constant Friend, mighty Deliverer, has taken its place — ever with us.

Once, indeed, we were in the seventh, but then we were at best only as servants in our own Father's house; but now we have — through faith in Christ — received the spirit of adoption, and have become in the fullest and happiest sense, sons and daughters of the Lord God Almighty. Then we feared before Him as servants in presence of a Master, but now we dwell in love with Him as children with an affectionate Father, and as the bride with a loving bridegroom.

Our bondage is gone — freedom has come. Our sighs have given place to joys — our fears to hopes. Our vain struggles to a sweet confidence in the strong arm and loving heart of Jesus."

Now how shall this contrast be made more striking?

The grand difference between the two classes is, that the one has and the other has not found Jesus, as a present Saviour from the present power of sin. The one still sighs in the bondage of the sad and sorrowful problem, Who shall deliver me from the body of this death?

While the other now exults in its blessed solution, giving thanks to God for triumphant deliverance already wrought, through faith in our Lord Jesus Christ.

This — but this also involves another grand difference which must not be overlooked in the contrast.

They of the one class have a Saviour in Jesus it is true — but he is a Saviour afar off — up in heaven, as they think of him, and not with them now here upon earth. While they of the other class have Jesus ever with them — a very present help in every time of need — a friend which sticketh closer than a brother.

THE CRIPPLE.

A poor youth came to the shores of America from Old England, a few years ago, bringing with him only the prayers of a devoted mother whom he left in the home of his birth.

His faith stood then only in the teachings of his mother. The living faith which is the vital union between Jesus and the soul he had not.

Falling in company with Universalists on his way westward from New York, his traditional faith was soon shaken from its sandy foundation, and then the legitimate fruits of his new notions about universal salvation were quick to ripen, and most abundant in fruitage, though, alas, their fruits were not very fair to the eye nor very sweet to the taste.

Bitterly did he rue it afterwards.

He fell into loose habits and loose company. The Sabbath was turned into a play day, or a work day, as best suited to his pleasure or his purse, and vice ceased to be contraband even. His feet were on slippery steeps, and swiftly sliding, when suddenly the Lord arrested him by a casualty from which he was saved alive by a singular — miracle, shall I say? Almost a miracle it certainly was.

At work on a frame, then in course of erection, his foot slipped — he tottered — reeled — fell, he was at work on the second story — and falling he was caught by a joist below. He fell backwards and the small of his back came upon the timber. He was taken up alive, but with little hope of his living a single hour.

His agony was awful, and as he recovered from the first stunning effects of his fall, his returning sensibilities seemed more and more alive to suffering every moment.

Nothing relieved him. The severity of his pain constantly grew greater for many hours. At last in the madness of despair, he sent for a quantity of whiskey, and drank enough, as he hoped, to drown his suffering, and let him die in insensibility — but it failed to intoxicate. Strangely enough, it gave the relief which all the physician's medicines and skill had failed to give, and he began to recover.

With the thought of recovery came also a review of his past life. Remembrances of his home and his mother came upon him, and now his life of dissipation, with the opiate of Universalism, which had lulled his fears of God and Eternity, was to him like a dream when one awaketh. He felt it to be all wrong, all false. He saw his delusion, and most bitterly lamented his folly and sin.

Weary nights and days he prayed and struggled for peace and pardon. Sleep seldom visited his eyes. Fears were his daily food. His cries prevented the dawn of the morning. His sins grew heavy — a load too great to be borne.

At last, one night, overborne with weariness, he fell into a troubled sleep, and in his sleep he dreamed.

He thought he had fallen into a ditch, not very deep. It seemed to him at first easy to make his escape, but when he attempted it, he sunk down deeper and deeper with each successive struggle, until at last he found himself sinking in the mire over his head, and just about to be drowned in the filthy waters of that horrible place.

Just then, lifting up his eyes, he saw stooping over him, the bending form of a strong man, with his hand outstretched to save.

"Oh that he would save me!" thought the young man, and he ceased to struggle to save himself. Then the hand of the rescuer grasped him firmly, and lifted him easily out of the mire, and placed him upon the bank of the ditch, and in a moment he had stripped him, washed him, and clothed him anew — and just then the troubled dreamer awoke from his sleep.

"Ah!" said he to himself, "I see. I see. l can never save myself — all my struggles are in vain, and worse than in vain. l do but sink deeper and deeper. Jesus must save or l must perish."

And Jesus did save. His feet were taken from the horrible pit and the miry clay. He was washed and clothed, and made happy in a sense of sin forgiven, and the hope of Heaven.

His spirits rose, and his health returned — that is to say, the health of his body, from the waist upward. From the small of his back downward he was paralyzed and shrivelled away. From his waist upward he grew fat and fair.

He applied himself to sewing for employment and for a living, and soon acquired skill to earn a fair maintenance, with something to give to the poor and to the treasury of the Lord.

He as happy until by and by thoughts of his desolation began to grow upon him. Others, God had set in families; to him this was denied. None would ever love him as he longed to be loved. He should never have wife or children bound to him by the tender bond of matrimonial or filial affection. His heart yearned for the endearments which he felt in his soul he was created to enjoy. And as the certainty pressed upon him that he could never enjoy them, his heart sunk within him and seemed to he withering away like his limbs.

" Alas! " he thought, "must it be so? Yes, it must indeed. None could ever love me as the bride loves her husband. l can never have one to love and cherish, as the bridegroom loves and cherishes the chosen companion of his life."

Again he became intensely wretched. His troubled soul denied him the embrace of even "tired nature's sweet restorer, balmy sleep," until at last, in sheer exhaustion, he fell into wakeful slumbers, and dreamed again as before. In his dream he seemed to be entangled in logs and trees, lying criss-cross over the ground in utter confusion, as they are sometimes found in our forests, where the hurricane has done its work, and made what is called a windfall — no tree left standing, but all blown down, one over the other, in all conceivable positions.

In the distance, he saw Jesus standing, and at once began struggling to make his way over the logs to the Master, but could not. He was foiled in every attempt, and at last gave up in despair; and then, looking up, there was Jesus standing with outstretched arms, before him. And O, so lovely and so loving. The Saviour clasped him in his arms, and spoke words of endearment, assuring him that he would be ever with him; would never forsake him, but love him freely, as the bridegroom loves the bride, and cherish him as his beloved forever.

He awoke, and behold it was a dream, and yet not all a dream. Thenceforth the longing of his soul for one to love him, and be beloved, was satisfied. Evermore Jesus was with him, the bridegroom of his heart:

THE INQUIRER AND HER WISH.

There came to a little meeting of those who had already learned the secret of living in the faith of an ever present Saviour, and of those who were desirous of hearing about it, a very lovely woman, a wife and a mother; a Christian for many years, and yet by no means satisfied with her state and condition.

But let her tell her own story. The opportunity was given; it was in the parlor of one of their number, and ladies only were present. She spoke with a pathos that touched every heart — "l have been many years a Christian; l would not give up my hope of heaven for a world. It is founded upon the precious blood of the Son of God. I have committed my soul to him, and I believe he will not forsake me in the hour of death, or condemn me at the judgment. And sometimes I feel him very near to me, and then I am very happy. No tongue can tell how sweet my peace is at such times. It passes all understanding. But then again my heart wanders from him, and I try to get back to him. I pray, and repent of my wanderings, and resolve to keep my heart more diligently, and promise the Lord if he will only restore me l never will wander again; but alas for me! too often all my resolutions and promises, and cries and struggles, are vain, and I am forced to give up and live on, conscious that l am left by the Saviour, so that I could repeat, with some sense of its bitterness, the agonized cry of the dying Redeemer himself, in the hour of his darkness: Eloi, Eloi, Lama Sabachthani! My God, my God, why hast thou forsaken me?

Now I have come here to learn from you, dear friends, if you will teach me, how to live so as to have my Saviour ever with me.

I am like a wife who tenderly loves her husband, and longs for his society, and would fain make his home so agreeable to him that he would never leave it for the club or the theatre, or the opera or a party, or any other place, however fascinating; but who, for want of wisdom or skill, so fails as ever and anon to be forsaken by him for a time, and for times that seem wearisome and long to her; and who is utterly at a loss how to change her own course so as to win and secure the constant presence of her husband at home.

Once I had a father — noble man — he is now reaping in heaven the reward in glory of a life of singular devotion to Jesus upon earth. He was a wonder to me. He seemed to have the presence of Jesus from morning till night, and from year's end to year's end, always from my earliest recollections. I do not remember ever to have heard him make the complaint made by so many, and alas! made so often by me — of the absence of Jesus. His face kindled up in a moment at the mention of Jesus, and all his prayers and all his words and ways showed that he was full in the faith of that assurance, "Lo, I am with you alway, to the end of the world."

My ease was so different that I often wondered at it.

One day, shortly before he took his triumphant departure to heaven — I was then about eighteen — I asked him, saying father, how is it? I frequently wander away from my Saviour, and find it hard to return. You seem always to have Him present with you. Do you never get away from Him?

"Never, my dear child, never; never so but what I can get back in one minute."

I shall never forget his words or his looks; and I have come now to meet you here, and learn, if I may, how to live always in the faith of the presence of Jesus as my beloved father did."

This secret of living in the faith of an ever present Saviour — loving, tender, watchful, faithful — is the secret learned by those of the eighth chapter class, and this is the secret of their zest in repeating the triumphant answer to the sad question, Who shall deliver me from the body of this death? I thank God through Jesus Christ our Lord.

And this is the secret which they, of the class of the seventh chapter, have not learned, and therefore it is that they still sigh in their bondage and groan under the weight of the body of death.

It is quite remarkable, however, that while these last point to the seventh of Romans as the exposition of their state and condition, they always clip this graphic chapter at both ends to make it suit their experience. It opens with the beautiful representation of the matrimonial relation as that between Christ and his followers, and closes with the exultant note of deliverance from the very state of bondage to which these sighing ones point as their own.

A moment's thought should make them see that they are not honoring the Bridegroom Deliverer when they point to this hopeless bondage; this struggling, sighing, groaning condition; this slavery to sin; this wedded state with a Body of Death as the Bridegroom — as the state and condition to which he has introduced them. A poor bridegroom, surely, he must be, who holds his bride as a slave, sighing and groaning for liberty, and crying out, Who shall deliver me from the body of this death!

And a poor bride must she be, whose heart goes abroad for its pleasures away from the embraces of her groom; so fascinated by the contraband delights of the world, that even when she would be true to her home and her spouse, she is always haunted by thoughts and desires after others!

Perhaps there is no more striking example of the contrast between the two classes, than that which is presented in the Bible between the two states of the apostles themselves, before and after the Pentecostal baptism.

Like the twelve found at Ephesus by the apostle Paul, if the question had been asked them before the day of Pentecost, Have ye received the Holy Ghost since ye believed? The appropriate answer would have been: We have not so much as heard whether there be any Holy Ghost. And like Apollos, before he was taken by Aquila and Priscilla, and instructed into the way of the Lord more perfectly, they had as yet only the baptism of metanoia conversion — a change of heart — and not yet a heart filled with the faith of a present Saviour, wrought in them by an indwelling Holy Ghost.

Those two disciples, on their way to Emmaus — O, how pensive! how sad and sorrowful is the thought of a Saviour, absent from them. They thought it should have been He that would have delivered Israel. But alas! he was dead — he was gone, and

Israel was not delivered. A Saviour passed away, mighty in word and deed, hut gone not with them.

O, how different from Pentecost onward. A Saviour ever with them. Mighty in word and deed, and always present. Always directing them where to go; always, in every moment of trial, putting words into their hearts which all their adversaries could not gainsay nor resist; always, in every temptation, making a way of escape; always hearing their cries unto Him; always giving power to their words, spoken in weakness; always gladdening their hearts, even in dungeons and in the stocks, and in the fires and under the scourge.

Paul and Silas, with their bodies lacerated, bloody, sore and stiff in their gore from the terrible scourge laid upon them each forty strokes, save one — thrust into the inner prison, and their feet made fast in the stocks; were yet happier there in their prayers and praises to a present Saviour, than the eleven were in their liberty and in their safety, with all the assurance that Jesus was risen from the dead which their own eyes, from seeing him, and their own hands, from feeling the print of the nails and the print of the spear could give them, while yet their faith was not sufficient to see and feel and know that he was present with them in invisible reality and power.

To know that Jesus is with us, and that He will keep us by His own power, and wash us in His own blood, and lead us by His own hand, and uphold us from falling, or lift us when fallen, and watch over us day and night — our Shield, our Friend, our Shepherd and King, our God and Saviour! O, this is the crowning happiness of the Christian's heart and the Christian's life in this the house of his pilgrimage! Give me rather to stand with the three in the furnace seven times heated, and the Son of Man with me there; or with Daniel in the den of lions, and Jesus with me there; yea, a thousand times rather, than to recline or walk, or feast, in the palace of a king, if the King of kings be not with me there!

From this contrast of the two states and stages of experience, as they affect the Christian in his own heart and life — giving to his course the cast of sadness and l sighing under bondage in the one case, and of exultant joys in the glorious liberty of conscious deliverance in the other — we must now pass to these things as they affect the Christian in the power of his usefulness as a soldier of the cross, and as a worker together with God in the spread of His gospel. But this must form the subject of another chapter.

Chapter Six - The Harmony

DANGER, DUTY AND DELIGHT: OR, THE CUMULATIVE PROGRESS, AND CUMULATIVE POWER OF CHRISTIAN EXPERIENCE.

The fear of the Lord is the beginning of wisdom."
"Thy statues have been my songs in the house of my pilgimage."
"Ye shall receive power after that the Holy Ghost is come upon you; and you shall be witnesses unto Me in Jerusalem and in all Judea and in Samaria, and unto the uttermost part of the earth."

The contrast drawn in the seventh and eighth of Romans, between the Law and the Gospel is strong. And just, too.

The law, to those who cling to it and reject the grace of God, hoping to be saved by their own merits and works, does work bondage and death.

While the gospel, to those who receive it does work liberty and life.

Nevertheless there is no antagonism between the two, but harmony rather, and union, and power in the union.

In the husbandry of the farm, the drill and not the plow, gives the crop. If the land were left as the plow leaves it, there would be no crop, but of thistles and weeds. The plow destroys every living thing, tearing all up root and branch, and burying all under the ground. While the drill plants the seed, and under the blessing of God, ensures a golden harvest and a full garner. The farmer might plow his ground ten times, or a hundred times over, and yet never have a harvest if that were all he should do. Nevertheless there is no antagonism between the plow and the drill. It takes both to make the land yield to the diligent hand its reward.

In the husbandry of the kingdom, the law is the plow, and the gospel is the drill. And the deeper the plow is put in the better the crop, provided only that the drill follows in due time, casting in seed in abundance.

It is in the nature of Christian experience to accumulate power as it progresses from stage to stage.

There are three stages of experience in the life of every one redeemed to God. Conviction, submission, sanctification. And there are three motives corresponding, by which the Holy Spirit germinates, advances and perfects the divine life of the soul — danger, duty and delight.

A sense of danger first startles the careless one from his senseless slumbers and arouses him to flee from the wrath to come.

A sense of duty next rises into supremacy and constrains him to submit his own works and ways to God's.

And at last a sense of delight in the Lord and his ways becomes the absorbing and dominant motive in the heart and life, perfecting obedience in love.

In each there is power, and all the power there is in each and in all is accumulated by him who gains all.

The second absorbs the first, and the third the second. The sense of danger seems to become lost when the sense of duty becomes strong, and the sense of duty seems in its turn to be lost when it is transmuted by the grace of God into delight. Nevertheless not a particle of either is lost.

Leigh Richmond began his course as a clergyman of the church while yet he was in his sins, and knew no better. After a time he was awakened to a sense of his peril and guilt. Then he began preaching in the power of his convictions, and his people were preached by him into conviction, and under condemnation like himself. There they stopped — he could lead them no farther. He had not found the way out himself. How should he lead others out?

A year or two afterwards, however, the way was made plain to him, and right joyously he entered it. Then at once he began preaching justification by faith, and his people were soon rejoicing with him in the joys of sins forgiven.

While under conviction, but yet unconverted, be had power to preach the terrors of the Lord, and used it — but no more. The grace of God which saves the soul from wrath, may have been to him as a sweet song in the ear, but it had no power on the heart, and neither had he power to bring it home to the hearts of others.

But by and by, when it was made of God to him the power of salvation, then it became a power to others from his lips, to break their fetters also, and fill them with songs of rejoicing.

Meanwhile Leigh Richmond lost nothing of his power in preaching the terrors of the Lord, by passing himself personally out from under their weight, but gained rather — for now in the light of the wondrous sacrifice made to redeem sinners from exposure to the wrath to come, he could weigh with a hand more just the inconceivable weight of judgment and fiery indignation to which they are exposed.

Just so it is when the Christian is led onward into the experimental knowledge of Christ as his sanctification; it gives him not only the power to witness for Jesus what he himself has found so sweetly realized to him in his own heart and life concerning the presence of his Saviour, to subdue his sins, and keep him through faith, in all the fulness of salvation from day to day — but his sense of the exposure of sinners to the wrath of God and the Lamb, and his sense of way of justification through faith in this Lord Jesus Christ, are also greatly enhanced; while at the same time his own love of Jesus, and love to those in peril of losing their souls, is increased a hundred-fold.

The advancing experience is not so much like a chain of equal links, added one after the other, but more like a tree in its successive stages of growth. Each stage of its progress not only sends its top higher into the regions of faith and hope, and its roots deeper into the fatness of truth and love, but adds, also in equal measure to the strength and body of all previous growth.

Felix Neff is a singular instance of the power of one who is himself under the terrors of a certain fearful looking for of judgment, to awaken others to their perilous exposure. From valley to valley he blew the trumpet, amongst the mountains as if he had just come down from the judgment seat — and it was not until after his strength was consumed by the fire of his zeal, and he had come down from the mountains to spend the mere wasted brand of his life in the genial clime of the plains, that hope sprang up in his soul — the sweet

foretaste of joys to come.

If Felix Neff, however, had first felt the fiery condemnation of the law in his soul, and then found the sweet peace of sins forgiven, before his mission in the mountains, his trumpet would have sounded as loud and clear, and far more sweet; and great as was his success, it would have been manifold more, and his life many years longer.

Dr. Payson was a polished and powerful shaft in the hands of God. Hundreds were saved by his ministry; but much of his strength was wasted, in what he saw afterwards to have been vain strugglings. Had he known to trust in Jesus for his own soul's sanctification, and for all fitness to herald the Saviour to others, not only would he have been saved what he himself said was wasted, but his life might have been spared long to the church, and his success, great as it was, increased vastly in its measure.

The cumulative progress and power of advancing religious experience, is like to what sometimes happens in oriental life, in social, civil and domestic relations. A prince takes captives in war. They are kept under guard and in chains. They are dragged at his heels to grace his triumphal return to his capital. He holds the power of life and death in his hands, and they tremble lest he should order them killed. His eye is taken by one of their number. He orders him to be loosed from his bonds, and clothed in the livery of his household. He is installed as a servant and treated with all kindness. He in turn is dutiful and true to his master. Day by day he wins upon the regard of the prince, and step by step he is advanced in position, until at last he comes to be the confidant and adviser of the prince, in all the affairs of his household and kingdom.

At first he felt hatred only toward the prince, and that the bitterest. Then he submitted, only because he must do it or die. But now there has grown up a sense of duty to the prince so strong and deep that, rather than betray the trust reposed in him, he would prefer to die.

By and by the prince's affections become more like a father's than a master's. He has no sons and one daughter only, a lovely creature every way worthy of her father's fondness, the pride and joy of his life. He reasons thus, "Who so faithful, and who so worthy in all my kingdom, as this my servant? Whom could I trust with the happiness of my daughter, and with the rule of my kingdom after me, so well as he? If it suits he shall have my daughter, and he be my son and heir." The arrangement is made to the joy of all parties. The former captive, a servant of late, has now become a son. The livery of the servant is changed for the habiliments of the prince. And in his heart where dread ruled at the first, and duty afterward, now love holds the sway. The interests of his father are his own, and in the house where once he was faithful as a servant, he now serves faithfully still, but no longer as a bondsman, but as a son. He knows and feels the power and authority of the prince as fully as when he himself was a captive in chains, trembling for fear of losing his life; and feels ten thousand times more desirous of sustaining him in his authority. And he knows and feels his own duty as deeply as when he was a servant in livery, and loves far better to do it. But superadded to these, he has now also the affections, and the position, and the interest of a son, in the house and the kingdom of his father soon to be his. The submission yielded in the days of his captivity, only because he must do it or die, he now yields with the cheerfulness of reverence and love. And the obedience rendered afterwards from a sense of duty is now given as the joyful service of filial affection, and honor — the pride of his life.

Just so it is in our relations to God; the submission and service which at the first was the constraint of fear, and afterward the award of duty, becomes finally, in the fulness of faith and the fulness of salvation, an oblation of gratitude, rising out of the golden censer of a sanctified heart.

This is the crowning glory, and the crowning power, too, of the Christian religion, and of the divine life in the soul.

Other religions may induce fear as strong as death, and desire to escape from the penalty and power of sin sufficient to lead men on to toil and torture; but it is the Christian religion alone which has power to convert bonds into songs, and duties into delights.

And now how is it that this transmutation is made? What is that power, better than the philosopher's stone or the lamp of Aladdin, which works this wondrous change?

We have seen already that it is faith.

Faith: which is the assured hope of a home eternal in the heavens, and also an assured knowledge of the presence and power of Jesus to deliver us from the dominion as well as the penalty of sin, and keep as by the power of God, through faith unto salvation. The very crowning thing which completes the fulness of this faith, is the apprehension, not so much of the certainty of final salvation, as the joyful confidence of the presence of Jesus, as a present Saviour from sin, and a present captain of salvation, to direct us and sustain us in every conflict with Satan, and in every effort to extend the Kingdom of God in the world. And this is the very gist of the experience sought to be illustrated and urged in these pages.

And now, again, what is the great power of the followers of Christ for the spread of his Gospel? The power TO WITNESS FOR JESUS. And this is at once the greatest and yet the simplest and easiest power given of God to man.

To witness for Jesus. To point to the Lamb of God, and testify that he does take away the sins of the world. To hail the Captain of salvation as a present leader and commander, and inspire others with the like faith of his presence and power.

The child may wield this power if he has the faith in its fulness; but the greatest giant of intellect, or eloquence that ever electrified men by the fire of his genius, and the flash of his words, will utterly fail of this greatest of powers if he fails of the faith.

When Jesus, just then in act to ascend up to his Father from the summit of Olivet, promised the disciples that they should receive power, after that the Holy Ghost should he given them — in the same breath he added the definition of that power, by foretelling its use, saying: And ye shall be witnesses for me in Jerusalem, and in all Judea, and in Samaria, and unto the uttermost part of the earth.

The grand work of the Christian in the spread of the gospel, is to witness for Jesus, to tell the story of the cross. But mark ye! And mark ye well! Not that alone. That would be the story of a dead Saviour. Ours, thanks be to God is a living Saviour, ever living to make intercession for us. The story of the resurrection and ascension must be added to the story of the crucifixion and burial. But mark ye again! and mark well! not this alone — this would be but the story of an absent Saviour — ours, to our joy unspeakable, is a present Saviour, mighty to save, able to deliver, from all the power of the world, the flesh and the devil. The story of Pentecost must be added to that of Calvary and Olivet — the story of the return of Jesus in omnipresence and omnipotence, by the Holy Spirit, to be with all his disciples everywhere, even unto the end of the world.

It is ours to witness for Jesus; but our testimony cannot go beyond our experience. With the apostles, we cannot but speak the things we have seen and felt; but the things we have not seen and felt we cannot speak effectively and convincingly. The Holy Ghost must first witness to us, before we can witness to others, the things of experience. The convinced soul, like Leigh Richmond in the days of his conviction, may testify for the law in its heart searching length and breadth, and the converted soul may testify for the gospel in its power to bring sweet assurance of sins forgiven and the hope of heaven, but it is only him who has also found by similar deeper experience the way of sanctification by faith, who can point to Jeans as the deliverer from sin in like manner as from its penalty.

And then, too, as we have already illustrated in each successive stage of advancement, there is new spring and strength of force given to all that has gone before.

In advancing we do not lose the things that we leave behind, as we press onward to the mark, but double the old store in gaining the new.

The apostles did not more than half understand the significance of all that Jesus was and said while he was with them in person in the days of his flesh. But afterward, when in the power of the Holy Ghost, he came to them and dwelt with them, and within them, from the day of Pentecost onward, then with all that was new to them, in this new experience of theirs, there came also such a recollection of all that Jesus had said and done, with such a new

fullness of significance in all, as made it all like a new story to them.

Luther and D'Aubigne; in their after and deeper experience, found the word of God illuminated anew to them, with a richer and fuller significance of truth and grace. The things they understood before, they understood better now; and the things that came home to them with power before, came home to them with a new power now; while at the same time they saw Jesus, and felt the blessedness of his presence and might now in a new relation entirely, viz. as their sanctification – and in all this they were witnesses for Jesus in the fullness of the new power received from God, in the new experience of his wisdom and grace in providing a way of escape from sin itself as easy and plain as the way of escape from the wrath to come.

This accounts for the new spring and power of usefulness given to these men. Useful before, they were a hundred-fold more so afterwards. Their knowledge of science was not extended. They were not advanced to new and higher posts of honor and power. Their positions and circumstances remained as they were before, but they had made new discoveries in the science of salvation, and gained new positions in the world of faith, and the fire was kindled in their hearts into a new glow of fervency and light. The waters of life came welling up anew in their souls, overflowing and flowing out in rivers, in their testimony, oral and written, from pulpit and press, concerning Jesus, to a sin ruined world.

And this accounts also for what we sometimes see – more wonderful even than the abundant usefulness of such men as these who stand in the fore-front of the line – the equally abundant, though less wide-spread and widely known usefulness of persons who from extreme infirmity or age might be expected to cease from their labors entirely:

MISS SUSAN ALLIBONE, for example. Though young, she was for years before her departure from life unable to work or walk, but she could testify for Jesus. As she was wheeled along the sidewalk in her little hand carriage, she could address the workmen and the wayfarers whom she met, in tones and words so tender and sincere, that they wondered at the gracious things which she spoke, and bore witness that she had been with him who is full of grace and truth. Their hearts were touched and moved more than by the most eloquent appeals of the giants of the pulpit. And from her hands the tract was never refused, nor yet the exacted promise to read it prayerfully, it may well be believed, often left unfulfilled.

And they who came to her bedside, as many a servant of God can testify, left it with new light in the soul, and feeling as though they had been privileged indeed beyond the common lot of man, quite on the verge of heaven.

And of her it may he said — as indeed of all who have advanced so far — that the faith of the presence of Jesus in all the plenitude of sanctifying power and sanctifying grace, was the crowning charm and crowning excellence of all. Self-emptied and self-abased, prostrate at the feet of Jesus, she looked up to him as her all in all, and in him, never absent, always present to her faith, she dwelt even in the midst of the deepest infirmities, and sometimes in untold agonies of suffering, yet always on the sunny slope of the hills of salvation, and like the tree of life, always bearing fruit in abundance, ripening every month and every day of the year.

Her memoirs have been written. As much may be said of...

AN AGED SERVANT OF JESUS

...whose record is on high, but whose good deeds have found none to chronicle them amongst men.

At eighty his athletic frame had begun to tremble under the weight of years, and his manly form to stoop a little — strange if it had not been so. His infirmity indeed was so great that his children would no longer willingly consent to his living apart from them or following his old occupation. "Father," they said to him, "you have done enough already. It is time you gave yourself up to rest. Come, live with us. Let us take care of you. Enjoy the freedom of all our houses. Go where you please and when you please, and be at home wherever you go. All we have is yours. But work no more, and live no longer by yourself."

This was kind and right. The old man loved his children, and was delighted with this new evidence of their affection for him.

But no. He would not consent to their plan. For two years more he remained in his own house, and kept up his occupation and his establishment in regular routine.

Meanwhile, however, he visited every family, prayed in every house, and talked personally with every man, woman and child, of a suitable age, in a circle of five thousand inhabitants, and many were awakened by his words. He established and maintained also, a weekly union prayer meeting, changing from house to house in a circuit as large as he could extend it. And this was the beginning of a revival which embraced all the churches, and almost every family in the town in its blessed sweep. And all this was after he was eighty years old, and so infirm that his children thought it unsafe for him to keep up his home and live apart from them.

At eighty-two they prevailed. He was constrained to yield to their affectionate urgency — closed his establishment, sold out, and went to make home with his children. Then, in another town, some forty miles from his former residence, he was thrown into a new field — not of rest, as his children had hoped, but of activity and usefulness. Looking about him he saw a population of twenty-five hundred or more, with all the usual church privileges to be sure, but without any one — really in the spirit of Jesus — to care for their souls. So in the faith of an ever present Saviour, he girt about him his coat, put on his India-rubbers, filled his pockets with tracts, refreshed his spirit at the foot of the cross, and started out on foot and alone. With his staff in his hand, trembling with age, he went from house to house, here again, as he had done before, in his former abode, until here again he had entered every habitation, and left there the impressive solemnity of his affectionate warnings and importunate supplications, upon the ears and hearts of every soul.

In this instance he was not permitted to see the fruits of his work in a general revival of religion, as in the other. Not however because it did not occur, but because he was taken home to his mansion and to his Master above, before the seed so abundantly sown by his hand had ripened into the harvest. His last visit made, his last prayer offered, in the last house of the whole, he went home to his daughter's to rest for the night, to enter next day as he purposed, upon a course of revisiting such families as he thought his services most needed in.

But his work of going about like his Master to do good was done. He lived many weeks, but went abroad no more while he lived. It was the writer's privilege to see him in his room after this but some while before his death. The interview will never be forgotten. The bowed and shaking form of the decrepit but noble old patriarch made an impression not to be effaced by time, or crowded out by the images of the multitude seen since, thronging the thoroughfare of life. But if his form impressed, his words were burned in. O how glowing! How more than youthful, almost heavenly in their vivacity and energy. They were all life. Jesus had indeed given him life in another sense than the one usually conveyed by the word — a life which only seemed the more intense as his frame wasted and chilled, and grew heavy with years.

"Ah!" said he, "for twenty years now I have thought it would be nothing to die, but gain. But I did not know. My peace was made. I had learned also that Jesus was my surety and trust for purity and spotlessness as well as for pardon. I was ready -- all ready, and waiting. And I thought that at the word, in a moment, when the summons should come, I could joyously strike tent and away. But no. I find it very different. Not so easy as I supposed."

"Ah! How is that, sir? You are not afraid to die?"

"No, not that! Thank God, not that! "

"What then, sir?"

"O, my brother, it is not striking tent, as I supposed, this dying is not. It is pulling down this old house rather piece by piece; and as the old frame gives way, torn brace after brace and timber after timber, apart, it is terrible. And yet even in this, thanks be to God, my Saviour is with me. He does not forsake me, and his grace is sufficient for me. Sometimes the cry will rise up, if it be possible, let this cup pass from me. Nevertheless, again, always the cheerful words, Thy will, not mine, be done, well up after the others, and all is hushed and peaceful." So this venerable man conversed, while I sat charmed at his feet.

Now what was it gave him such a power to bring forth fruit in old age?

Five thousand people visited after he was fourscore years old, and twenty-five hundred more after he was fourscore and two. What was the power? I asked him. He told me. Let his words to me, as well as I can remember to repeat them, reveal his secret to all.

"I was converted young, in the place of my birth. For forty years I was a member of the church, and a Christian, too, as I verily believe, without ever having been the means, so far, as I know, of the conversion of one soul, and that, too, through all the prime and vigor of my youth and manhood, from twenty to sixty. Sometimes, when I think of it, I am overwhelmed with grief and shame. But I knew no better. I lived as others in the church did. Kept up all the duties of religion at home and in the church; kept Sabbath, prayed, read my Bible, went to the Lord's table, fasted when fast days were appointed, and sometimes when they were not, and often enjoyed the communion of the Spirit and the fellowship of Christians, and the adoption and heirship of a child of God; the Spirit witnessing with my spirit that God was my Father; thankful in prosperity, sustained in adversity, and comforted always by a good hope of glory; and yet, as I said, never in all that forty years, so far as I know, the means of saving one soul — (and here tears stole down his furrowed cheeks, the silent witnesses to the sincerity of his deep-toned regrets, and as he proceeded, there was indescribable impressiveness in his manner: sweetness, solemnity, tenderness, made his words thrill the heart-strings like an angel voice.)

At last, when I was sixty years old, God was pleased to visit the people of Utica, where I lived, in such power as I had never before seen. Hundreds and hundreds were converted — some from amongst the most hardened and desperate of the people, and others of the most moral and regular. There was a great shaking, too, amongst Christians. Scores gave up hope; concluded they had been deceived, and came out and took the position of newly awakened sinners, inquiring what they should do to be saved. I myself was seized with conviction — not that I was not a Christian, but that I was a useless cumberer of the church; a barren fig-tree in the garden of God; worse, it seemed to me, than any unconverted sinner in the world. Forty years of the prime of my life spent in the church and in the nominal service of God, and yet nothing done for the cause; not one soul won to Jesus. O, the thought was too bitter too bear. It bowed me down as the sturdy oak bows under the power of the tornado. Sometimes it seemed as if it would kill me outright; and then when I thought to make amends by a life devoted earnestly to doing good, then Satan taunted me with the idea that it would be a mockery to offer the decrepit and broken remnant of a misspent life to God, and ask him to use me in my old age to save others.

But he could not keep me from making the offer of myself to the Lord. Now, however, the struggle did but just begin; for in my first attempt to benefit others, my own heart, or rather want of heart, was revealed to me, and in the next effort the conviction of my utter unfitness was deepened, and so on and on, until the weight of my burden was not so much my past barrenness as my present unfitness to do anything more than I had done in the past.

Then came the temptation to stop, and say, "Ah! I am not fit to do anything for God; I was not made for it; and if I was, I have lived so long with using and improving my talent, that it has grown rusty — too rusty ever to be used." Satan here again, often taunted me, saying, Too old to change! Fool to think of it! But he did not stop me. My convictions were too deep; my burden too great; I could not stop. The thought of it was worse than the thought of death. And then something whispered hope to me, and I determined never to stop. Then I cried unto God, in my distress, to give me His Spirit and strengthen me for His service. But I cannot tell you the hundredth part of my struggles and troubles. Resolutions proved vain and cries for the Holy Spirit no better, at last, one day, for the first time in my life, I saw that the work of making my heart right, and keeping it right for the work of the Lord, was Christ's, by his own presence in the power of the Holy Ghost not mine at all. Christ's to save, mine to trust and to serve.

From that hour I left the Saviour's work in His hands to do, and looked to Him to do it, in the fullest confidence that He would; rejoiced that it was in such good hands — so trustworthy, loving and true — and I was not disappointed. From that hour I found it easy to wear the yoke and to bear the cross; and to the praise of God's own condescending love be it said, He has blessed me in His service and prospered me in the work given me to do. Jesus has been with me every day, now these twenty-two years; and every day I have done, in my imperfect way, just the work of the day, as my Saviour has laid it out for me. And one thing I can tell you, my brother, if I have been the instrument of good, it has been the Lord with me and this Lord within me who has done it, and not I. If the truths concerning Jesus has been in me, at well of water springing up into eternal life, and a fountain from which streams of life have flowed forth, I have been no more than the earthen pitcher which carries the water, or the iron pipe which conducts it. The power is of God. To God be all the glory. He alone is worthy to receive honor and power, and might and dominion; and He alone shall have it forever and ever, Amen."

Such was the story of this aged disciple, ten times over more touching and impressive from his trembling lips, and sunlit tear-bedewed face, and speaking eyes, than from the cold pen that writes it.

As he ceased, reflections and questions came crowding up; but a moment only was left before the car-whistle must be obeyed, and the venerable man left to the quiet and peace of solitary but blessed waiting for his summons in turn.

Some word was dropped about it, and the old man's thoughts flew onward and upward. "Ah! yes," said he, "this is my depot; I have come to it at last. Here I am, and here I wait. How long, my Father in heaven only knows. But not long. The bell will soon ring — the rush and roar of the train will soon be heard — the sound of invisible pinions. The summons will be given. Not in the shrill voice of the steam-whistle, but in the voice of angel song, or sweeter still in the voice of Him whose words are as the sound of many waters, and as the sound of tens of thousands of harpers, harping with their harps. Ah, I long to hear it; I long to see my Redeemer; I long to be with Him where He is, and behold His glory."

O, what a lustre, as of heaven reflected, shone his face! Within myself I said, Happy, happy, happy man! Thou indeed hast found not the fable but the true fountain of life! Thou hast stooped and drank of its waters, and eternal youth is thine! I could almost, without qualification, have applied to him the prophetic address to the Messiah, then yet to come, made by the Psalmist hundreds of years before His coming, " From the womb of the morning thou hast the dew of thy youth." So youthful was the spirit, so full of the freshness of hope and the vivacity of joy that still lingered and clung to the old tenement of clay.

To me he seemed like a young and beautiful bride, brought by her beloved and loving spouse into an old mansion, crumbling into dust, and ready to tumble before the first gust that should come, but brought there only to wait until the new and noble mansion, built and furnished by the hand of provident love, should be ready to receive her; and she, ready by contrast to appreciate it, when the time for "flitting" should come.

But that which impressed itself most deeply of all, was the contrast between the forty years of barrenness, the forty best years of his life — from twenty to sixty — and the twenty-two years, the two last years above all of such noble fruitage to God. Forty years without the known conversion of one single soul, from his influence, and the two years after he was eighty, hundreds converted. Ah! here was a contrast to be pondered well by one like me.

And the cause of it, too. Faith — the faith which accepted the command — Go ye!— that emphatic first clause of this great commission — Go ye! and obeyed it.

And the faith which accepted also the promise in both aspects — the present and the future — Lo! I AM with you always, and Lo! THOU SHALT be with me where I am to behold my glory.

His was the faith already spoken of before — the faith which gives all and takes all, and therefore has all — and all in Christ — whom having, there is nothing more it can ask.

In parting with the venerable brother beloved and father revered, one word was dropped to try him as to the source of his complacency, whether it was in himself or in Christ. May it be forgiven if even in the slightest shade of ap
pearance it was wanting either in sincerity or respect.

Grasping his hand with the warmth of true admiration and love, (he returned it with interest,) I said, "Well father, I must leave you to wait here in your depot for the celestial train that will take you home to glory, and go myself to meet the earthly train that carries me back to my field of toil. You are all ready, and waiting." This was said in the deepest sincerity, and the response was, "Yes, thank God, all ready. Ready, and longing for the summons."

"You have done so much for the Master and his cause, and experienced so much, that you will not be ashamed to meet him and be ushered into the presence of the Father and of this holy angels."

Looking me earnestly in the face, while a shade of sadness and surprise came over the brightness of his countenance, he grasped my hand and pressed it more warmly than ever, and then placing it between his two, as if to impress the truth upon me with a double power of pathos, he answered:

"No! No, my son, not that! not THAT! All I have done is nothing — all I have experienced nothing. I am nothing. My righteousness is as filthy rags — at best no better than the torn, tattered, defiled, crossed, condemned notes of a broken bank. It would be an insult to offer it. It would be madness to trust to it. No! no! no! my son! Thank God I have a better hope. Jesus is mine and I am his — and that is enough. He who has been with me through every trial in life will he with me in death. His grace will suffice. I shall not be ashamed to meet him, for he has bought me with his blood, and sealed me by his Spirit. And I shall not be ashamed to go into the presence of his Father and my Father, for he will change me into his own heavenly image of spotless glory, and being like Him I shall be like all who are His. Jesus is all in all. Good by — may Jesus go with you, and be with you evermore."

So we parted.

Chapter Seven - Gathering Power of the Church Foreshadowed

Instances like the octogenarian, with the den of his youth, and more than the vigor of his prime and like Carvosso, made eminent by grace; and the African woman, greater in her poverty and sickness than the Hon. Judge in his health and his wealth, are types — very imperfect ones, certainly — foreshadowing the power and blessedness of the whole church of the future.

Happily, too, the growing shadow of the incoming glory, indicates the time when all shall have the fulness of this experimental knowledge of Jesus, as at hand.

There is one movement of the times which must strike every reflective observer; it is this process of POPULARIZATION. God, in his providence, is spreading the treasures of knowledge and power amongst the people. Everything, in every department of human acquisition, which has hitherto been kept within the narrow circle of the limited few, God is now opening out to the millions. He is making the masses rich; lifting them up; and ennobling them in every element of true greatness. There are 'prentice boys, this day, who know more than Franklin did of the workings of the fiery fluid, brought down from the clouds by him, and had they lived in his time and known what they now know, their memories would be lifted up to lofty niches in the temple of fame.

Many a lad in the engine works, taking the early lessons of his trade, knows more of the power and application of steam than Watt or Fulton knew; and many a schoolboy is better acquainted with the order, numbers, magnitudes, distances, motions and laws of the heavenly bodies than Copernicus. Really, these school-boys and 'prentices and greatest in these elements of greatness, than Franklin, Watt, Fulton and Copernicus.

Knowledge is popularized, and knowledge is power. But the best of all knowledge is the knowledge of Jesus, and the greatest of all powers is the power of God through faith in Jesus, and this knowledge and power are being popularized.

The question is often asked, Why does not God raise up some Whitefield or Luther in our day?

The answer is, He is raising up a multitude of Whitefields and Luthers. He will have all men to be Kings and Priests. The same great truths which made Luther and Whitefield great, will soon make the whole church of Christ upon earth, a church of Whitefields and Luthers;— if not in intellect and eloquence, yet in living union with Jesus, which was the greatest and noblest endowment of these noble men.

This popularizing process is universal. It goes forward in everything. Not alone in the utilities, but in the luxuries and elegancies of life. "Costly apparel," such as once must be sought alone in king's palaces, finds its way now into the cottage. Silks, satins, broadcloths — where will you not find them? The servant does not wait now for the cast-off clothing of master or mistress, but buys new from the shop, more showy, if less costly, than their employers wear. Gold chains, once the ornaments of the princes of Mammon, now festoon the persons of the servants of tradesmen. Travel — formerly the rare privilege of this favored few — is now enjoyed beyond the sea, to countries remote, by flitting, migrating myriads; while at home, the whole people, drones only excepted, like bees of this hive, sip nectar and gather manna from every flower, and every pool too, alas, in the land. Coach and livery are distanced out of sight, and almost driven from the track by the iron-horse and his train; and he and his owners care little who rides and pays; whether plebian or prince. Even the light and the lightning are harnessed in for this process of popularization. Turned artist, this light paints our likeness in a few seconds for a few cents, with truthfulness which, if it does not flatter like the pencil, never lies. And so it comes about that these facsimiles of our loved ones, ere-while the rare and treasured ornaments of mansions and palaces only, are now piled up in every cottage. And the lightning, tamed and taught — not the English — but a universal language, is turned spokesman for the world; and soon, if not already, will so speak as to be heard, whether in behalf of king or peasant, the whole world over in a single moment of time. It is, therefore, just in harmony with this universal movement, that God is also popularizing the deeper and sweeter knowledge of Jesus.

A scene occurred one morning in far-famed Old South, Boston, in the morning meeting in the chapel, too natural to be noticed as at all extraordinary by the attendants at that precious daily reunion. At the close of the meeting, after the sound of the Doxology had ceased its hallowed vibrations, as the people were greeting each other, and leaving the chapel, two of the venerable men always occupying the front seats, with their ear-trumpets upturned to catch every word, arose and greeted each other. One placed his trumpet to his ear, and turned up its broad mouth toward his stooping white-headed companion. The other, bending down and almost burying his face in the open mouth of the trumpet, with a show, loud, waiting utterance, said, "Well — brother — we have been long — meditating — thinking — trying — to find out how — this divine life —could be best promoted — in the soul — and — we shall get it yet! Yes, we shall find it yet!"

"O, yes, yet! We shall — we shall!" was the answer.

Yes. Yes, venerable Father! Even so. You will very soon. The Master will soon call for you and then you shall see Him, and He is the "best way," the only way. God grant, however, even now, before ye shall go hence, that Jesus may reveal himself to you as the best way.

In that same assembly, a moment before its breaking up, a fair-haired youth arose and said, " Dear brethren, help me to praise God! I have found this way! Jesus is the way! He is mine and I am his! He is complete, and I am complete in him!"

Here were the venerable fathers feeling after the better way, and here was the child in it already, happy and satisfied.

Leaving that sacred place and falling in with one of the dispersing worshippers — " Ah my Brother," — so was the greeting —"You seem to understand that Christ is all in all. Your remarks show that you are in the light. "

"Ah yes Brother. Those words of Dudley Tyng stand up for Jesus — and those other words, 'Praying IN Jesus' — as his father has published them to the world, came home to me like a new revelation. I have long been a Christian, and an active one, but the life hidden with Christ in God, I never understood till then; but since then my views have been all new, and the fire has burned in my heart as it never did before."

Introduced to one in the meridian of life, who had been many years bearing his part in a prominent city church, he began talking of Jesus and what the Saviour had done for him. "O His ways are wonderful. He has dealt with me in great wisdom and mercy," said he. "I had a lovely wife. She was the sunshine of the house — and we were the happiest family in the world — so we used to think and say. But God came and took my wife away. My children felt it deeply. I was inconsolable — all summer I went mourning and bowed down. Life was a dreary waste. I thought I should go down in sorrow to the grave. But I was led to make a new covenant with the Lord, and somehow, I can hardly tell how, Jesus manifested himself to me as the way, and now all was new to me. The Bible was new. The Christian life was new. The world was new. And I am happier now than I ever have been in all my life — happy in Jesus."

And he is not alone in his church. Others too, have come out in the same fulness of light. And yet others are feeling for it.

After an address to S. S. Teachers, closing with the thought that the well-spring of power to the workers for Jesus is union — an abiding union with Him.

"That is it! That is it!" said one of their number. "That is the very thing. O for that living union with Jesus."

At the parlor fire-side, half an hour later, in the sweet home of another of the teachers addressed. "You touched the spring of all power," said he, "in the closing remark."

"Yes," responded his excellent companion, "I have felt it for years, and longed to have the experience of it myself. My husband has been deeply interested a few months now, and now do tell us How is it?"

Here too, another yearning heart was found — one who is a missionary among the Indians. She had left home, and friends and all, to go and tell the Indians of Jesus.

Her life was laid thus a living sacrifice upon God's altar. She had tried the work and loved it, and longed to be worthy of it. And now, while home on a visit, hearing one and another speak of a new and higher experience, she grasped at it in a moment, as what she needed to satisfy the cravings of her own soul, and also to give her a higher power of usefulness in her mission.

"Tell me," said she, "all about it. I must have it, but how? It is wrapped all up in mystery to me. I long to have it explained."

In another place, one who had been some while enlightened, and been a living witness, testifying the things that Jesus had done for her, and how precious he was to her every day, and all the time, said, —"Come and see us. There will be gathered at our house tomorrow evening, the parlors full of those, either recently come out into the fulness of faith, or seeking instruction as to the way."

These are the incidents of a few hours, and they are given to show a little of what comes to the star-face in the view of a single observer, of the great work, going on, deep down in the solid and substantial stratum of the church, hidden almost entirely from the eye even of the Christian world.

So God is popularizing this union — this abiding vital union of Christians with Christ.

So also, is it in the field of activities as well.

The attentive observer cannot fail to see that the church is in the transition of a new phase of its life and power. The Philips and Stephens are multiplying; but what is most remarkable is to see the privilege of actual usefulness grasped by so many who have thought hitherto they could do nothing. Young men, business men, maidens, mothers, clerks, apprentices, journeymen, firemen, and even those who have run after the firemen — in some instances outstripping even the watchmen on the walls — and this increasing every day.

Prayer and exhortation come from the lips of those in all grades of the church, from the youngest to the oldest, and in the tones and words of glowing hearts and fire-touched lips. The old man no longer says, "I am a dry tree, I cannot bear fruit." The youth no longer says, "I am untutored, I cannot speak." The businessman has ceased to plead, "I am busy, I cannot spare time." All come up, and all come up to the help of the Lord. This at least is the tendency of the present, and in this there is a prophecy, that all will come up in the future at hand, if they do not already.

And O, of the power the church will have then, we can form no conception! Isolated cases of the power of abiding union with Jesus and its blessed abundant fruits, do certainly give some idea of individual power; but then these are isolated cases, and isolation is weakness, combination is power.

A thousand grains of powder, or a thousand barrels if you please, scattered a grain in a place and fired at intervals, would burn it is true, but would produce no concussion. Placed together, however, in effective position, they would lift up a mountain and cast it into the sea. Even so the whole church filled with faith and fired by the Holy One who gave the tongues of fire on the day of Pentecost, will remove every mountain, fill up every valley, cast up the way of the Lord, and usher in the jubilee of Redemption.

Something of this power we may see in such instances as the great awakening.

What was the secret spring touched by the Lord a hundred years ago to throw open the doors for the reception of Jesus by the tens of thousands then converted to God? Just this very experience of full salvation in the leaders and others.

What was it by which the Lord prepared Edwards, the Wesleys, and Whitefield, to herald the blessed Jesus to the multitudes with such simplicity and power? Just this very experience of full salvation.

What was it that gave Luther power to break his own Roman fetters, and become the champion of the free? Just this experience of the power of Jesus in him for full salvation.

What was it that gave the apostles power to come forth into the light themselves, and shed the light in such effulgence upon a benighted world? Christ the Sun of Righteousness risen in their own souls.

And if in the past this has wrought such glorious things by the few, and the isolated, O, what will it not work when it shall pass into the experience of all?

Christ in the church, walking in invisible power amongst the golden candlesticks — Christ seen by the faith which is the evidence of things not seen — Mighty to save!

And the world seen in its guilt and peril!

Death at hand. The Judgment near. Heaven and Hell — with the impassable gulf between — opening to receive the crowding multitudes who are hasting onward!

Ah! When these great realities shall become the realities of living experimental apprehension, then will the church arise for the conquest, and then shall the battle be fought and the victory won.

There is one way in which we may shadow, dimly to ourselves, the power of the church, then. Suppose every church in the world revived at the same moment, greetings from the north and from the south and from the east and the west, coming in from every city and towns and hamlet and habitation, "The Lord is here!" "the Lord is here!" Then suppose that to go on from year's end to year's end unceasingly — no longer in spasms, chills and fevers no more alternating, but ever and ever the Lord working His works; sinners seeking and finding the Saviour; Jesus the hope of glory — every man's theme!

Ah! that would be glorious!

But even then, you must add the higher element of power. Jesus our sanctification, filling every man's cup of blessedness to overflowing, before the picture is complete.

When Jesus was on the earth in person, and the people saw him with their eyes, and heard him with their ears, they thronged him, and wondered at all his mighty works. Then he was only in one place at a time. The economy of God for the future is that of the presence of Jesus in all the plentitude of his grace and power in every place at the same time; working works of salvation more wonderful than miracles, and his presence realized by faith so that it is really substantial; that is actual.

In the days of His flesh, even his disciples failed to understand the nature of His kingdom and the glory of His designs. God's economy for us in the future is that we shall be strengthened with might in our hearts, that Christ may dwell in us by faith; that we, being rooted and grounded in love, may be able with all saints to comprehend the length and breadth and depth and height, and to know the love of Christ, which passeth knowledge, and to be filled with all the fulness of God.

Then, when this is the status of universal experience, and when Christ is realized as present in every church, working in power, not limited by unbelief, as it was in the days of His flesh, and when the cry of every church is, the Lord is with us! The Lord is with us! and the glory of every soul is Christ the hope of glory — then will the church come up to its normal state and to its predicted efficiency. And then a short work the Lord will make of it in the earth. For then he who stands out against the power of truth and grace will soon be cut off by the righteous hand of unsparing judgment. Amen. Even so come Lord Jesus. Come quickly. Amen and Amen.

Chapter Eight - Closing Counsels and Parting Words

THE WAY OF PROGRESS. DANGERS AND DIFFICULTIES

A fourth part should, of right, be added, if our limits were not already reached. Many practical questions of deep and general interest, such as growth in grace, discipline, temptations, self-examination, watching and prayer, reading, study of the Scriptures, methods of doing good, and the like, might well form the conclusion of a work upon experimental religion.

However, if we must leave these topics untouched, it is a consolation to know, that whoso shall find Christ in His fulness, and dwell in Him, will live in Him, and in His Word, and His Spirit, counsel and strength which no work of man — no human hand or human heart could give.

At best, authors or ministers, are but like the finger and the tongue of John the Baptist pointing to Jesus — always present — as the Lamb of God that taketh away the sin of the world.

We must get beyond the minister, however wise and good he may be; and beyond the book, however full and clear its teachings, to find Jesus. The Song of Songs, which is Solomon's, gives the truth in words of honied sweetness, when the bride is made to say...

> "I sought him but I found him not:
> "I will arise now and go about the city in the streets,
> "And in the broad ways I will seek him whom my soul loveth:

"I sought him but I found him not.
"The watchmen that go about the city found me: —
"To whom I said, Saw ye him whom my soul loveth?
"It was but a little that I passed from them;
"But I found him whom my soul loveth.
"I held him and would not let him go."

Ah! when we find him, and while we will not let him go there is safety, progress, happiness, usefulness, for us. Satan cannot lay hold on us.

A little child, who was told by her mother that the tempter could not get her, because Jesus would be with her, answered, "Why, mother, I am in Jesus!"

We are in Jesus, if we abide in him.

Therefore it is that exhortations may be dispensed with, because abiding in Jesus we shall be watchful and prayerful, diligent and faithful, secure from the adversary and cheerful as the lark.

Like jets and chandeliers connected by hidden pipes with the great meter at the works, our light will burn on, and shine evermore, because Christ is our unfailing fountain head.

He in whom Christ dwells by faith will pray with all prayer and without ceasing, because prayer has become his vital breath; and like the beating of his heart and the heaving of his lungs, his soul will go out in prayer and praise, spontaneously without the lashings of conscience and the urgencies of duty. Songs in the night will come welling up from the overflowing joys of his heart; and his very dreams will take on heavenly hues and shapes.

He will be active. The spirit in him will be love; a constraining fire in his bones; he cannot but be active. He will be generous. If he abide in Christ — who, though rich, for our sakes became poor — himself the free gift of God to us — he cannot but give freely for his Master and his Master's cause.

He will grow in grace; for he has a living union with Him who is full of grace and truth; and from Him he will receive grace for grace.

He will have no longer occasion to examine himself to see whether he is a Christian at all or not saying and singing the mournful strain,

"Oft it causes anxious thought;
Am I his or am I not?"

For he will have left the dim line of uncertainty so far behind in his race, that his days of groping will be ended forever. His examinations will be to see whether he is "in the faith:" abiding in Jesus: not lifted up, not turned aside, but in the fulness of the faith.

He will press for the mark; for every day the mark of the prize will brighten and swell out toward the proportions of an actual presence, a substantial verity; and every day his urgency will accelerate, as on eagle wing he mounts up toward the goal of hope.

But what is it to abide in Jesus?

To abide in Jesus, is just to keep always the very attitude taken when Jesus was accepted.

As ye have received the Lord Jesus Christ, so walk ye in him — rooted and grounded in him, saith the apostle.

We received him very humbly. We felt our place to be the dust. Our righteousness to be rags. Our power to be weakness. And looked to Christ for all things.

Even so abide. So walk ye in him.

He who is lifted up with the idea of some exalted state of purity, or power, or safety gained, has in so far forgotten the apostolic injunction and is not in the lowly way where Christ was received by him. His joy is in his state, not in Christ. His trust is in his own attainments, not in Christ.

The command is not — Now you have got into a high and holy state, so walk in that; but even as ye received CHRIST JESUS, so walk in HIM.

One who had found the blessed Saviour by faith, and had his eyes opened to see the folly of his blind struggles to gain the goal by works: — became so enamored of faith, as to think of that night and day, and extol it to all listeners. But his comforts began to fail, and his light grew dim. His soul pined away into leanness again, and grew hungry, he could not tell why. By-and-by, however, a beam from the Sun of Righteousness dispelled his darkness. He saw that he had magnified faith instead of Christ. Just as if one should look at the system of iron pipes underlaying the city streets, and conducting the waters into every house, and forgetting the fountain, which supplies them, should say —"Ah, it is these pipes which bring their crystal streams to all! We owe all to these pipes."

Satan even tempted him to question whether, the power was not in the faith itself independent of Jesus. So that if there were no Saviour, yet if faith could be the same, whether the salvation would not be received. But even while he questioned thus, the power began to wane, as the supply of water in our houses would begin to fail, the instant the fountain head was shut off from the conducting pipes. And it was only when he returned again to Jesus as the fountain which supplies the Waters of the River of Life, that the streams began to flow again in full current into his heart.

We received CHRIST AS ALL-SUFFICIENT, even so let us abide in Him.

FATHER A--------

A venerable and lovely Christian, instructed in the way, but trembling and hesitating whether, after all, it would do for him to trust in Jesus alone, without some sign or seal of his acceptance, arose in a social meeting and touched every heart by the childlike simplicity, and lucid clearness in which he set forth the way, and the humility with which he confessed his own past mistakes. Then in conclusion he said — "But now as for me, I see that the only way is to trust in Jesus. Every other Way has failed me. I have no hope in anything else. I see that it is His to save me from my sins, just the same as it is His to save me from hell. And I know He is able to save to the uttermost. But — but — whether He will do it — for me — I — I — dare not say."

He resumed his seat, and for a moment breathless silence reigned. Then another arose and said, "Father A. reminds me of the counsellors of Washington at the Brandywine. The American army had crossed the bridge, and were going on to meet the enemy. Washington called a council. His officers assembled. He proposed the question, 'Shall we burn the bridge?' They said, 'No — we may want it to retreat over.' Washington overruled them, saying, 'Burn the bridge! Then there will be no retreating!' So the order was given, 'Burn the bridge!' and the bridge was laid in ashes."

The brother was going on to apply this to Father A., but he sprang to his feet, exclaiming, "I'll burn the bridge!" And he did. From that hour he was a living witness, and a lovely one, too, that Jesus is the way. All sufficient without signs or anything else to Him who receives Him.

That's the way! Burn the bridge! Leave no retreat! Venture wholly.

This we have done — if we have — done it. Even so abide in Christ. Wholly in Him. Always in Him.

Suppose comforts fail, light grows dim, clouds arise, the heart becomes laggard, courage sinks, joys fall into the sear and yellow leaf — or begin to, what then?

Fly to means? No — fly to Christ. Christ is what we want. Christ is all we want. Having him we shall have light, comfort, courage, joy and everything — without him we shall have nothing.

Suppose you were in a church or hall at night. The lights were dim. Hardly light enough to make the darkness visible. And suppose you should see the sexton busy, working away at the burners, trying to enlarge their apertures of escape for the gas, to increase the light, and all the while you know that the gas is partially shut off, in the pipe connecting with the main, and that is the reason of its faintness in the jets.

You will go to him saying, Man! Man! let the jets alone! Go turn on the gas from the main! Then let him do it, and instantly the room is full of light. Every burner does its duty. Ten to one he will have to go round to each burner and reduce the light to keep it within bounds.

Even so every man who has full and abiding union with Jesus will do his duty. His light will shine, and he will rather need restraint than spurs and goads.

"I am the door," said the Master. We all believe that. There is no other.

But the same lips said these other words, "I am the way," and this is equally true. There is no other. Practically, many believe in Jesus as the door. By him they enter the gateway to glory — and then, too, they expect to be met at the end of the way by angel messengers, and ushered into the presence of Jesus. But between whiles, they expect to journey in the straight and narrow way by virtue of their own resolutions and watchings, with such help from God and man as they can secure from time to time.

Lame faith! O what a wretched life of ups and downs they have of it, living in that way.

O that they only knew that Jesus is the way. He not only offers to be with them the pillar of cloud and of fire, the manna and the fountain, but he is The Way and there is no other. There is no real progress heavenward but IN JESUS.

Abiding in Him.

One thing more — vital to this abiding union with Jesus in its fulness: that is a constantly renewed consecration to do his will.

"If ye keep my commandments ye shall abide in my love: even as I have kept my Father's commandments and abide in his love."

It is an every day freshness of full purpose to do all the will of Jesus, that is here enjoined as the way to abide in his love.

Every day the panorama of life shifts its scenes indeed kaleidoscope-like, our circumstances change to the turn of every moment, almost.

Some disciples think they must look over the ground of duty at the end of each year, and begin anew on New Year's day. Most of those who pretend to serve the Master feel it incumbent when setting out in the world for themselves, or when commencing married life, or when engaging in a new business then to seek a new adjustment to their new circumstances. But this should be the daily, hourly, constant manner of the disciples of Christ. "I do always the will of my Father," said the blessed Saviour, "and if you will keep my commandments you shall abide in my love, as I have kept my Father's commandments and abide in His love."

Just here many and many a truly converted one has missed the way and slid into darkness.

There is no living in the light without living in obedience.

Remember! Faith accepts the command and obeys, just as it also accepts the promise and rests upon it.

The branch abiding in the vine, adjusts itself to the times and seasons of the vine. It puts forth buds, blossoms and leaves in the spring, fruit in the summer, and in the fall ripens its precious burden for the husbandman, then drops its leaves, and composes itself for the rest and strength-gathering time of the winter. Just so we need to adjust ourselves to the will of the Master daily and hourly.

So shall we abide in his love, and so shall his love also abide in us forever.

Before closing, there is one practical question — always important, doubly so now — concerning young converts: What shall we tell them?

Shall we tell them — as alas, is too often done — Ah, you are joyous now, but your joys will soon fade?

No. That would be cruel, even if true; but it need not be true. Tell them rather — Abide in Jesus, and your joys shall be full.

Tell them like Paul to press for the mark, and like President Edwards, to be more urgent in seeking the Lord than before conversion, and then with Paul you shall be filled with all the fulness of God, and with Edwards your joy in God shall be so great that when you walk in the fields everything shall be alive with God, and you shall not be able to speak forth his praises — your swelling emotions will seek expression in song — his statutes shall be literally your songs in the house of your pilgrimage, and as your joys so also shall your usefulness be. The joy of the Lord shall be your strength. You shall be abundant in labors and abundant in success.

But what shall we tell the young convert about the higher life?

Tell him that he must go through a long process of seeking — must try all the by-ways before finding the highway? No. No.

Tell him simply to abide in Jesus. As he has received him, so to walk in him. Give himself to Jesus, soul, body and spirit.

Commit the keeping of his soul to Jesus.

Commit the purifying of his soul to Jesus. Commit all the affairs of life to Jesus. Cast all his cares upon Jesus.

Take Jesus as all in all, and find all in him. Take up every cross. Keep every commandment and walk in his love. Tell him to do this and he shall not grope in darkness, but will be in the higher life —

"And all that life is love!"

Tell him the words of Jesus.

"I am the true vine, and my Father is the husbandman. Every branch in me that beareth not fruit, he taketh away: and every branch that beareth fruit, he purgeth it, that it may bring forth more fruit.

Now ye are clean through the word which I have spoken unto you.

Abide in me and l in you. As the branch cannot bear fruit of itself, except it abide in the vine: no more can ye, except ye abide in me.

I am the vine, ye are the branches. He that abideth in me, and I in him, the same bringeth forth much fruit: for without me ye can do nothing.

If a man abide not in me, he is cast forth as a branch, and is withered; and men gather them, and cast them into the fire, and they are burned.

If ye abide in me, and my words abide in you, ye shall ask what ye will and it shall be done unto you.

Herein is my Father glorified, that ye bear much fruit; so shall ye be my disciples.

As the Father hath loved me, so have l loved you: continue ye in my love.

If ye keep my commandments, ye shall abide in my love: even as l have kept my Father's commandments and abide in his love.

These things have I spoken unto you, that my joy might remain in you, and that your joy might be full."

Tell them further from Jesus —"This do, and the 'promise of the Father' shall be shed upon you, and 'Ye shall receive power when the Holy Ghost' is given you; then shall ye be 'witnesses unto me.'"

And now, unto Him who is able to do exceeding abundantly above all we ask or think, according to the power that worketh in us, unto Him be glory in the church, by Christ Jesus, throughout all ages, world without end. Amen.

Made in the USA
Columbia, SC
11 June 2021